THE END OF PRINT

First published in the United
States in 1995 by Chronicle
Books
First published in the U. K. in
1995 by Laurence King
Publishing

Copyright text © 1995 Lewis
Blackwell   design © 1995
David Carson

Library of Congress
Cataloging-in-Publication
Data:

Carson, David.
   The end of print: the
graphic design of David
Carson / by David Carson,
Lewis Blackwell.
      p.cm.
   ISBN 0-8118-1199-9
   I. Carson, David—
Themes, motives. I.
Blackwell, Lewis, 1958-
   II. Title.
NC999.4.C375A4 1996
741.6'092—dc20
                  95-19296
                       CIP

Printed in Italy
Color reproduction by Global
Colour, Malaysia
previous page illustration:
vera daucher

Distributed in Canada by
Raincoast Books
8680 Cambie Street
Vancouver, B.C. V6P 6M9

10 9 8 7 6 5 4 3

Chronicle Books
85 Second Street
San Francisco, CA 94105

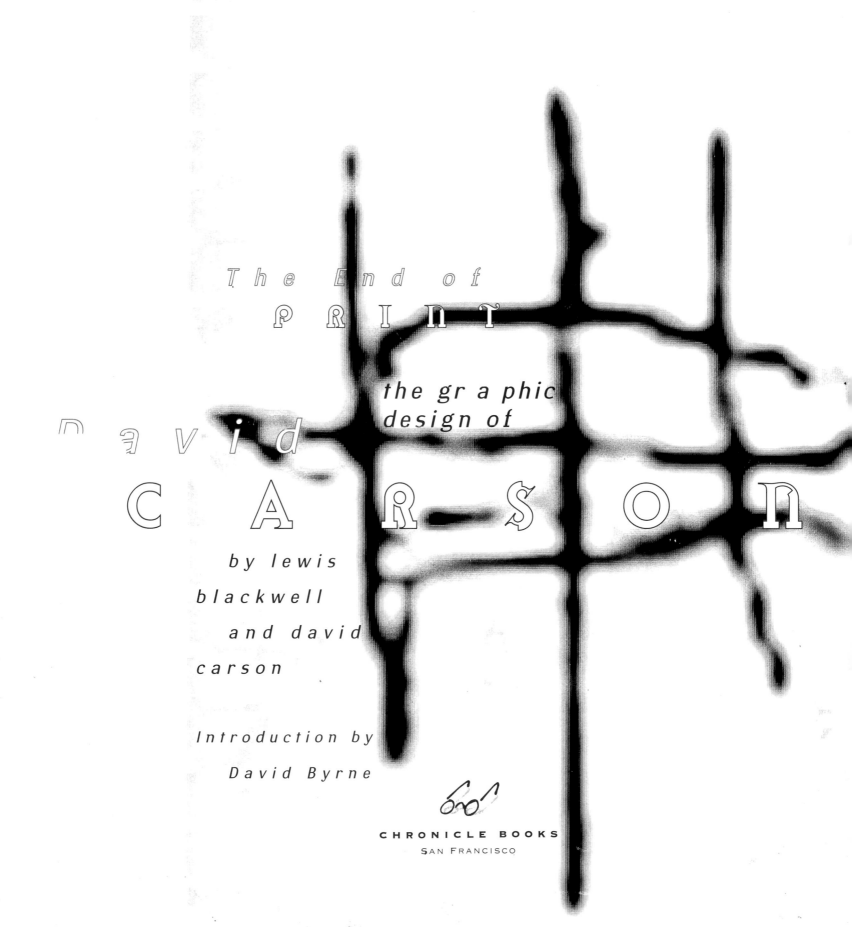

The End of
PRINT

David

the gr a phic
design of

CARSON

by lewis
blackwell
and david
carson

Introduction by
David Byrne

CHRONICLE BOOKS
SAN FRANCISCO

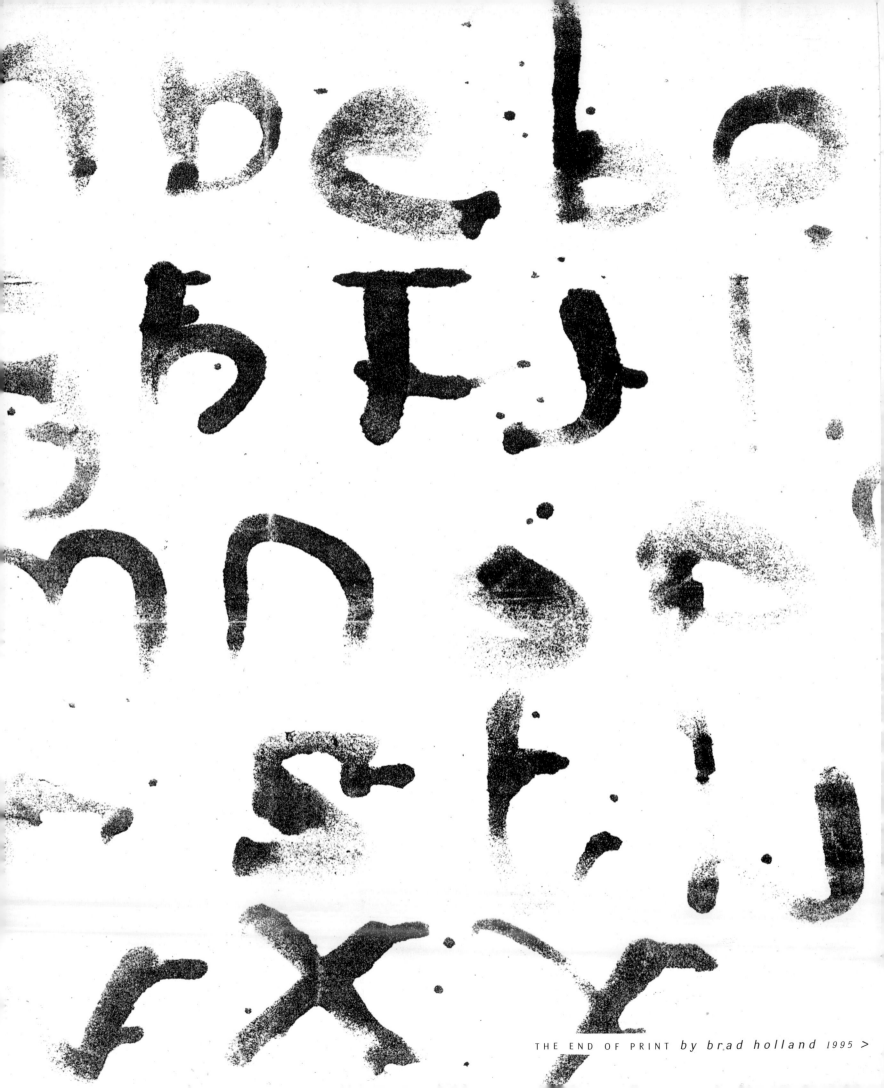

THE END OF PRINT *by brad holland* 1995 >

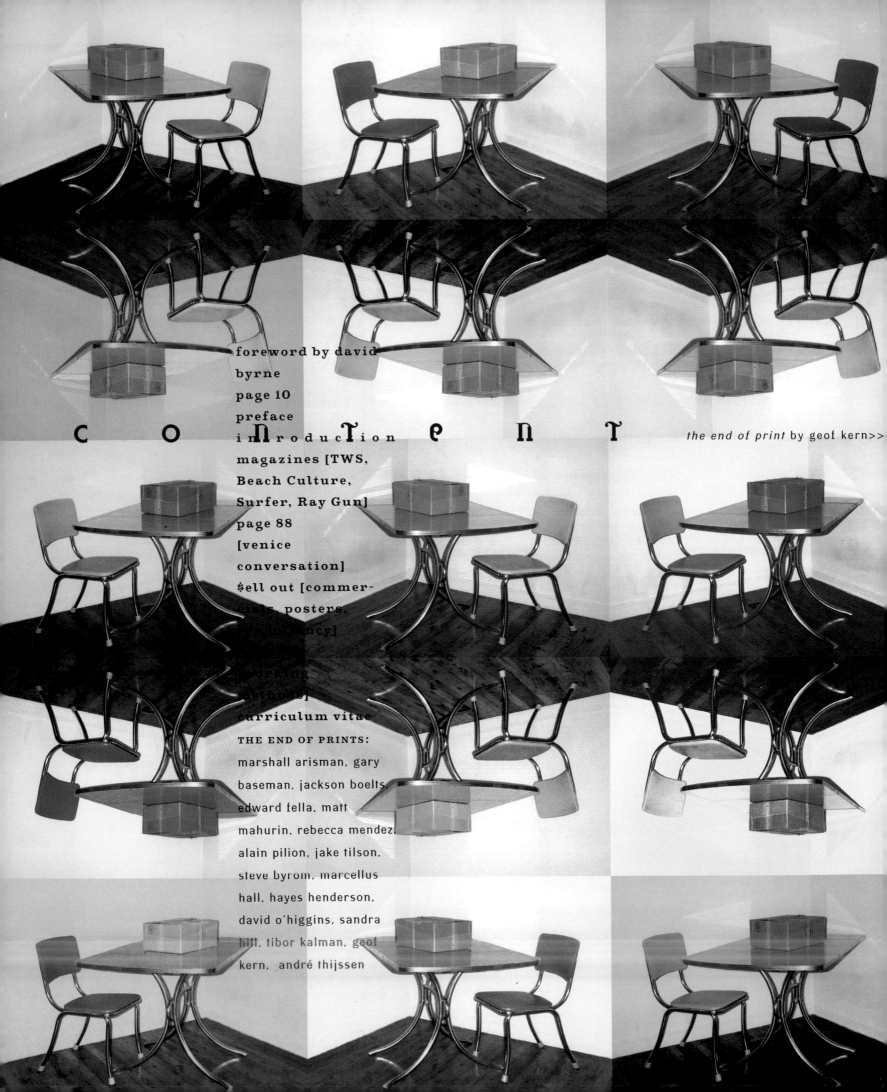

c o n t e n t

the end of print by geof kern>>

foreword by david byrne
page 10
preface
introduction
magazines [TWS,
Beach Culture,
Surfer, Ray Gun]
page 88
[venice
conversation]
$ell out [commer-
cials, posters,
consultancy]

[working
methods]
curriculum vitae
THE END OF PRINTS:
marshall arisman, gary
baseman, jackson boelts,
edward fella, matt
mahurin, rebecca mendez,
alain pilion, jake tilson,
steve byrom, marcellus
hall, hayes henderson,
david o'higgins, sandra
hill, tibor kalman, geof
kern, andré thijssen

I first saw David Carson's work, as did a number of others, in the short-lived magazine called Beach Culture, and I immediately wondered what the hell was going on. Who was reading this amazing magazine that seemed to be in the wrong place, directed at the wrong audience? It seemed to act like a popular mag, but sure didn't look like one. Were surfers really into this radical design? Were they actually more savvy than I gave them credit for? Well, Southern California was the home of Kustom Kars and Low Riders, both examples of beautiful, radical, impractical design of and by the people. Maybe this was another step along those lines? Popular culture proving once again that it could be more revolutionary than high culture.

Then Beach Culture disappeared and we never found out the answers.

I was beginning to despair that rock music culture was becoming square, conservative, stuck. The mass-market mags were all towing some kind of party line, getting excited when they were supposed to, and narrowing their interests and focus until the world started becoming a suburban backyard. And that was what we were trying to escape from!

Then along came Ray Gun, and hey, it's that guy again! Now we're talking!

Design was cool again! Suddenly, visual expression was, as we always knew it was, as hip as Rock & Roll. Even the readers were contributing great drawings, paintings and sketches. This was not an isolated designer freaking out, but a catalyst for who knows how many people who knew that there is no difference between anything anymore - between "professional" musicians/artists and amateurs.

For decades, public art programs have tried to "bring art to the people"; museums and great institutions of learning strive to "enlighten the masses". When all along the "masses" have been doing it for themselves - maybe unrecognized, and in slightly different forms. With guitars and offset fanzines. With kustom kars, surfboards and skateboards.

I suppose a lot will be made of David Carson's work being the perfect example of McLuhan's theory of sprung life - that when a means of communication has outlived its relevance, it becomes a work of art. That print-books, magazines, news-papers will become icons, sculptures, textures - that they will be a means of communication of a different order, and that simple information transfer will be effected by some other (electronic) means. Print will no longer be obliged to simply carry the news. It will have been given (or will have taken, in this case) its freedom, and there is no going back. Print is reborn, resurrected, as something initially unrecognizable. It's not really dead, it simply mutated into something else.

David's work communicates. But on a level beyond words. On a level that bypasses the logical, rational centers of the brain and goes straight to the part that understands without thinking. In this way it works just like music does - slipping in there before anyone has a chance to stop it at the border and ask for papers.

-**david byrne,** nyc, 1995

the end of print *BY MATT MAHURIN*>

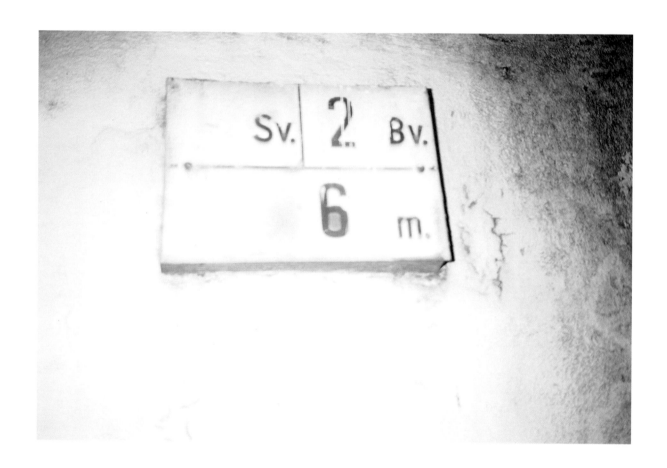

is a vital means of expression. At least to the end of this book.

One day ink on paper may be marginalized as a source of information, but for the foreseeable future it

For now, print is as relevant as you find it: in that you are reading this, it would seem to be working

communications.

aries.) Print and broadcast media are under pressure from the digital, online media that are reshaping

Carson's work celebrates this uncertainty of knowledge, ceaselessly questioning and revising bound-

media, not replaced. Or perhaps not. If we know one thing, it is that everything changes. (At one level

are seeing the emergence of a new graphic language in print, stimulated by the developments in other

ing with the pieces at the end of a spent culture, but rather signs of a new understanding. Perhaps we

Perhaps the strange new configurations of information in Carson's layouts are not some decadent play

of a dying culture. But can we claim "the end of print", when there is more of it than ever before?

One direction is hinted at in the title of the book: it suggests these designs are experiments at the edge

tions as emblems of our age and consider where mass-communication is heading.

seems to be a movement. It is that which makes the case for this book. We can look at these construc-

music have at times worked for or with Carson. He is in the vanguard, out there riding scout, on what

many other respected and innovative artists across fine art, photography, illustration, advertising and

young designers who have found in the work a convincing new take on how graphics can communi-

c a t e

find some new messiah to lead them through our media-rich age. However, it is not only stu-

dents and

Of course, his disciples may only follow through a desire to reject the advice of their teach-

ers and to

preserve the structures in which they have been comfortable.

the ways in which he has cracked the apparently flimsy edifice of design "rules", his opponents seek to

leading to wild acclaim from some and savage criticism from others. While his supporters appreciate

ic arts. His work has explosively challenged treasured conventions concerning the handling of content

But while pioneers can be heroes, they can also get shot at. For some, Carson is a criminal of the graph-

he has opened up new territory for the graphic designer.

aries of invention. In cutting up, layering, disrupting and distorting (and often not) words and images

enough area in which to experiment, yet Carson has somehow reached beyond the acceptable bound-

recently by his work for a wider range of clients in publishing and advertising. It would seem a safe

He has done this by, initially, the striking originality of his designs for niche magazines, followed more

tors in the world, the most closely-watched by his peers. And perhaps the most vilified.

an unknown designer of a short-lived specialist magazine to being one of the most awarded art direct-

of graphic design" with "deliberately senseless" art direction. In five fast years he has gone from being

our subject, David Carson, that he is "the master of non-communication", a man who "breaks the laws

Ah yes, the layout of a magazine. How could such a small thing provoke people to make remarks upon

cuts of a television commercial or the layout within a magazine?

rubbish in the gutter, the security cameras on a building, your home, the high heel on a shoe, the hot

What else takes responsibility for the values represented by the look of the exhibition in a museum, the

Every society gets the visual environment it deserves. Doesn't it?

"10" by doug aitken. background: found art from
L. Porter's print shop. san diego. 1995

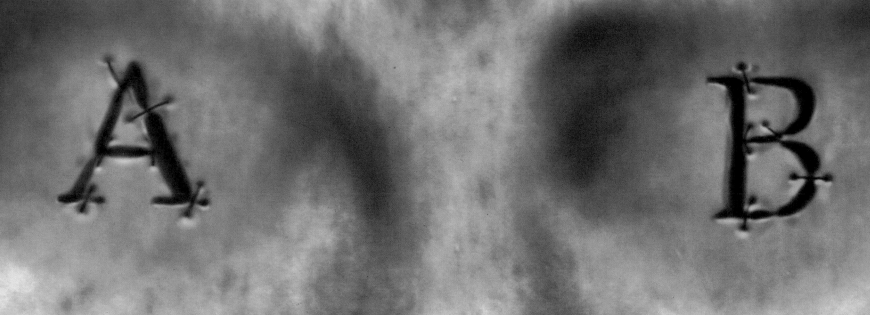

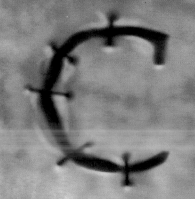

Uncertainty ... These pages of pages. Even when empty they are still the ... you to impute some

it is worth remembering that ... here with expectations. these are unavoidable. ... Uncertainty rules in these pages. These pages of pages. Even when empty the subject then in general ... know which language to they are still there, saying something ... waiting for you to impute some assume, that the leaves will need turning, that the beginning is at the front, purpose. and so on. these are assumptions, not rules or laws. it is not necessarily it is worth remembering that as you will have come here with expectations. our intention to fulfil these these are unavoidable. the expectations must exist, if not specifically of ¿CONFUSED? THERE ARE PICTURES.¡ the subject then in general of a book you will know which language to these pages, people are trying to communicate. They range from assume, that the leaves will need turning, that the beginning is at the front, spokespersons of youth sub-cultures to the advocates of corporate America easily and so on. these are assumptions, not rules or laws. it is not necessarily Diverse our intention to fulfil these. as the subject matter, circumstances and clients involved may be, they have all done

the end of print <BY MATT MAHURIN

¿CONFUSED? THERE ARE PICTURES.¡

Behind these pages, people are trying to communicate. They range from

spokespersons of youth sub-cultures to the advocates of corporate America. Diverse

as the subject matter, circumstances and clients involved may be, they have all done

dc/ david slack

this through the conduit of David Carson's imagina-

tion. He
is there as the art director of articles and photographs; as
the commissioner of illustrations in magazines; as the
designer of some of the very characters of the typeface or
calligraphy; as intermediary of the advertising message,

moving pictures and type within tight confines of

meaning in order to extract some new inflection on

the

brief and a revised relationship with the consumer; as

the creator of 25 frames per second that test our

or as the maker of
eyes' responses to television;
books, of this page.

Aristotelian stella

shawn wolfe

† SECRET MEMOIRS OF
A RENAISSANCE POPE †

The work evades capture within a set of rules about **"what is good design"**. The work doesn't   ,   ther does its maker. In the numerous interv   talks, wo   and other public explorations of his id   s in the past thr   ur years, Carson has declined to arrive   t some pat stateme   tent that may be used as a broad interpretation of the wo   ad, he prefers to let it stand on its own terms, piece by   and admired [or rejected] by those it was aimed   g he likes others to show what is in them, ques   work which reflects his own or the styles of others.   lection of new artists, there is a tendency to admire the n   e; in his commissioning of estab- lished illustrators or photographers, there is a tendency to offer these artists the freedom to e   eriment, to break from the stric- tures that are normally   on a brief. In the same way that he refuses to give him   clusive structure, or acknowl- edge the theoretical framewor   s and critiques applied by others,

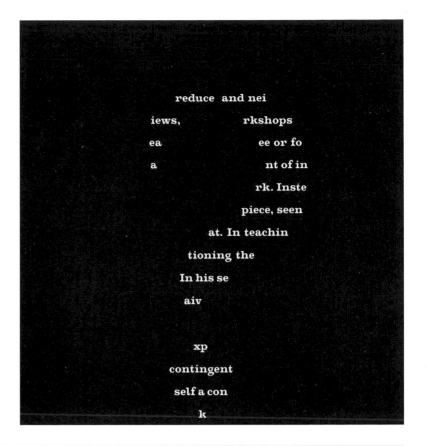

reduce and nei

iews,   rkshops

ea   ee or fo

a   nt of in

rk. Inste

piece, seen

at. In teachin

tioning the

In his se

aiv

xp

contingent

self a con

k

bob carson. grants pass oregon. 1995

it's
always
been
True

arrival of major advertising briefs,^{including work}
on a Budweiser Super Bowl commercial this
year,points to a breakthrough into mainstream
mass-communication. The work is no longer a sub-
culture,it is the cutting edge of the leading communications culture. Now where
next, with all those people watching?¶This book
addresses the question of how Carson's ideas work
in mass-media,suggesting they go beyond style. We
have to look at the means and motivations by which
they exist to see that there are ideas at work that
lock into our desire for both immediate and complex
interaction with the media. This pairing – immediate
and complex – is almost a pair of opposites in terms
of putting across an intelligent message,but it is one
grappled with by mass-communications every
day,every hour. Carson has taken this tense relationship and forged a new amalgam of graphic
materials in order to withstand the strain.¶We have
laid down an extensive route through Carson's projects [although it still shows only a fraction of the
material created for the magazines]. Behind this
tour are two intentions. Firstly,seen together the
work suggests its own evolutionary principles,from
the late 1980s to the mid 1990s. Secondly,it provides
a real portrait of the artist,if not the theory of the
art. For the latter,there will be plenty of clues for
the construction of

[your own theories.

Outside of the readers of Ray Gun, there has been
little mass-distribution of the work: Carson's early
layouts on Transworld Skateboarding, Surfer and
Beach Culture magazines are still being discovered
[and sometimes cannibalized]. His more recent

**so he passes this attitude on to his collabora-
tors and followers.
At these various points – in designing, commissioning, teaching,** speaking – he betrays
what could be described as an expressionist
approach, if a label is requireD .his work is full
of devices that visualize an emotional and non-
figurative, non-literal response to a brieF .but
the expressionist tag is likely to be as misleading as it is helpfuL. while he admires artists
such as mark rothko and franz kline, both key
participants in the heyday of american abstract
expressionism, so he also draws on other art
forms, from street imagery and elsewherE .he
doesn't become a musician or a documentary
artist as a result of these influences, so it would
also seem sensible to beware of too easily
labelling the work expressionisT .[A tag which,
after all, can and has been applied to much of
2oth-century Western art.]

set   left,   wh te   m vement

¶the difficulty of categorizing and the lack of an
off-the-shelf theoretical standpoint has both
helped the Carson culture and has hindered it.
While some may seek out the work,all the more
convinced by its avoidance of categorization,so
others can chafe over the lack of an expressed
unified theory,sneer at the unconventional aspects
of the work **and dismiss them as irrational gimmicks,**at best the fashion
**of the moment. Such negative reac-
tions are to be found within some
parts of the small world of design
critics,**plus the odd elder of the
graphic design community. To the
**broad mass of creative profession-
als,**to the lay reader coming to this
work fresh,the initial reaction is
one of surprise,perhaps shock,and
**almost definitely curiosity. Albeit
Carson has been working in a dis-
tinctive vein for more than five
years,**until recently it was in spe-
**cialist markets and he relied on
design awards to give the wider visi-
bility. But the growth of Ray Gun magazine,**the

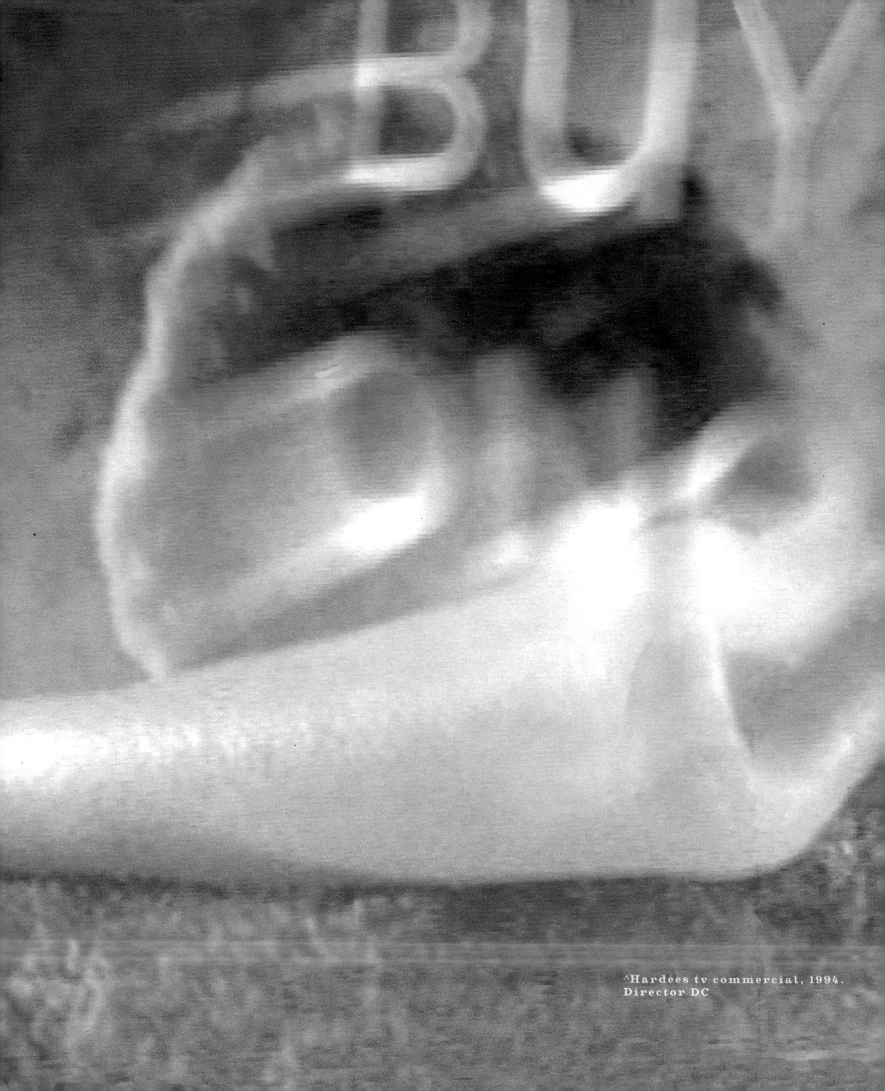

^Hardees tv commercial, 1994.
Director DC

TV Guide tv commercial, ^ 1994.
Director DC

contributions to advertising campaigns for major clients around the world, both in print and film, are at once projected to millions, but also prey to the ephemeral lifespan of advertising.

This book at last gives a considered record of the work and provides some explanation. It also takes on the challenge of the comment by the designer Neville Brody [Creative Review, May 1994] that Carson's work signals "the end of print", a comment that has continued to resonate since.

But before you can have a response to that provocative description, there is a need for some questions to be answered. As a result, much of the text in these pages asks questions [the title itself is really an implied question]. Some of these questions others have asked of Carson and have either failed to get answers to; or have asked and have failed to publish the answers; or are questions that have not been asked but where the answers have been assumed, perhaps mistakenly. In the Venice interview these inquiries are renewed and responded to at length.

For now, let us consider a general, catch-all question that seeks to sum up [or perhaps introduce] the puzzle for many in looking at the work. I could put it like a design critic: "Is there really a coherent set of principles behind this work?" Or I could just ask:

IS THERE A POINT TO THE DIFFERENCE?

The answer is throughout the book, but it can be answered simply here.

The answer is "yes".

But don't expect those principles to be set down in a row, with points of difference itemized and explained.

For one thing, the attacks on convention in these pages are not done with a consistent armoury of weapons. Neither are they done from one standpoint: the artist evolves with the work. For

craig allen

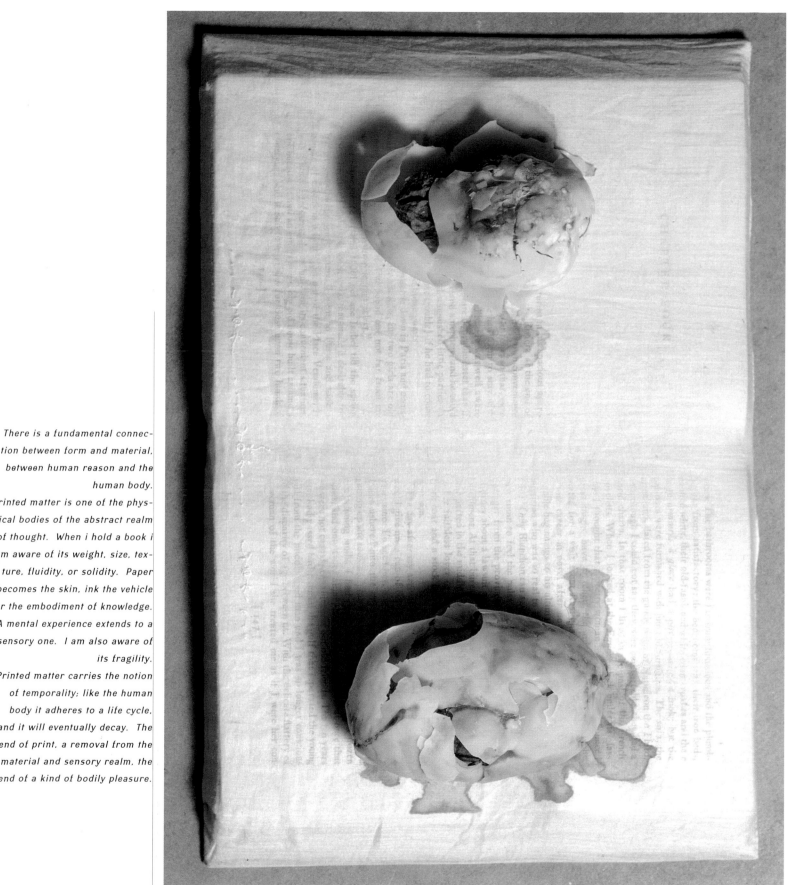

There is a fundamental connection between form and material,
between human reason and the
human body.
Printed matter is one of the physical bodies of the abstract realm
of thought. When i hold a book i
am aware of its weight, size, texture, fluidity, or solidity. Paper
becomes the skin, ink the vehicle
for the embodiment of knowledge.
A mental experience extends to a
sensory one. I am also aware of
its fragility.
Printed matter carries the notion
of temporality; like the human
body it adheres to a life cycle,
and it will eventually decay. The
end of print, a removal from the
material and sensory realm, the
end of a kind of bodily pleasure.

the end of print(image + words) BY REBECCA MENDEZ 1995

example, the fact that the layouts of Beach Culture and Ray Gun have no discernible grid, doesn't mean that they would always reject the grid. They might be freeform, but that doesn't make it a rule. Sometimes when a pattern seems to be emerging, it will be disrupted [as within the pages of Cyclops, where an overall restrained style is arrived at by an approach to the typography that consistently shifts in font, scale and positioning]. There simply isn't a system to be taken apart and detailed. There is not the reductive methodology of the Swiss style school of graphic design, or of the teachers at the Bauhaus, or even of the more recent Deconstruction graphics theorized out of Cranbrook [even though some might misleadingly associate Carson with some of those designers].

The lack of a big theory, of a rulebook, doesn't necessarily mean the work is intellectually unsound, or that its freedoms imply chaos. But it does mean that it consistently challenges and never arrives at a situation where there is a complete, common understanding of the thinking behind the design.

Consider: this book is readable, as are the magazines. The fact that not everyone feels comfortable with them is inevitable, but that is a problem faced by each and every communication. But in contrast to the manner in which much mass-communication seeks to reinforce shared understandings, adopting familiar constructions as vessels for content, here there are highly individual responses, every piece of design being uniquely expressive of the content, being part of the content. The overlapping structures, ad hoc logic, sympathies of image and word – these and other devices seek out and connect in different ways with the readers, enriching the initial content, be it an article, set of pictures, sheaf of letters, or other. Instead of a system, the design takes place more organically. And the connections change not only in the internal logic of the resulting images, or word-images, but also in how they connect with the viewer/reader.

This lack of set-down principles is contrary to the mainstream,

conventional awareness of innovation in design. Even some supposedly radical designers can be related to a movement, an area of thought. Carson's work could be seen as related to the burst of typographic experimentation that came out of some of the colleges and was associated with certain magazines in the late 1980s. But it won more fans and awards and upset more people than the likes of CalArts or Cranbrook students' work and picked up wider and more mainstream attention than the activities of, for example, the experimental type magazine Emigre.

Perhaps because the design community could once again

L.A. car shot, dc

focus on a personality at the centre of the work, rather indeed like the attention Neville Brody received in the 1980s, so Carson has come to be seen as the leading figure in a movement of graphic expressionism, or the dean of deconstruction art direction. He wouldn't want either title. While he may be in a leading position, he has never worked, taught or published in a way that could be seen as setting himself up as a leader of any group or tendency; indeed, it is remarkable how cut off in some ways he is from other parts of the design community, working out of a small studio in San Diego, southern California, previous to which he worked from home in Del Mar, just north of the city. It's not exactly Alaska, but it is away from the centre, out on the edge of the country, away from any regular group or design scene, such as exists in New York or London. Carson relies on telecommunications, freeways and airlines to reach his clients and to fulfil the requests for his lectures and partic-

car photo:dc. typeface"mani-
sto" by vera daucher +francis
ebbing

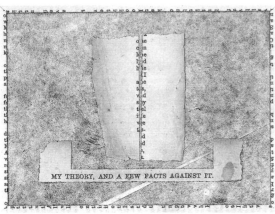

MY THEORY, AND A FEW FACTS AGAINST IT.

ipation in work-shops. Any evangelizing he does is through *the appeal of his work in the magazines, books and advertising. And all of these outlets for his expression are commercial enterprises, unlike the output of design schools and theoretical magazines, which exist to serve themselves as much as a separate audience or a market.*

Despite the "real-world" production of this work it has often upset those who stress that design should "function". It clearly does function in some regard, otherwise Carson wouldn't have any clients and his magazine art direction wouldn't last beyond one issue. But the chief thrust of the criticism would seem to be that function in graphics requires that it carries either obeys established, agreed principles, on its surface an explanation of any that it radicalism.

IT WOULD SEEM THAT GRAPHIC DESIGN IS OFTEN EXPECTED TO BE TRANS-PARENT OR FLATTERING OF A VIEWER'S PREVIOUS EXPERIENCE AND VAL-UES, OR BOTH. If a new approach is proposed then it is expected to announce itself with a declaration of intent, outlining principles rather than just doing it. Carson has consistently

challenged this with work that does not acknowledge the theories. Despite finding a resonance in his targeted audiences [the readers of the magazines and books, the viewers of the advertising], this has not held back critics from suggesting the work is in some way wanting.

[something else to think about]

We are seen as being at the end of the age of enlightenment. These days are the age of uncertainty, of doubt, where we are losing our confidence in understanding the world by a remorseless scientific process of hunting down truth. Space programmes and nuclear technology were perhaps the final awesome flowering of the quest for

rationalism that began with the Renaissance. Now, instead of sharing principles of discovery, we are struck by the conflict of our theories, along with the conflict in politics and the revival of religions [itself a sign of that loss of faith in science]. Perhaps it was always so. This uncertainty extends to our media. We don't know how we may communicate in the near future. ¿Will we all be on the internet? ¿Will we have portable phones wired to our ears? ¿Will computers be packed into what used to be a wristwatch? Whatever, we cannot assume books, journals or even television are lasting media: they are increasingly seen as way-stations alongside the superhighway to an interactive future. Such technology is with us now: we, as a global com-

munity, just have to choose.

In-this=context,what[logic]lies;behind
accepting$the°hollow+structures:of—designers past?Their/grids,their·
neo-classical-this=and[that,their-
isms?You]can<accept$them;as°something+to:hold—on·to,or·
y o u = c a n [l o o k
for]a;new$way°of+seeing.Look:for—a·new-structure:for[our
visions]of;the=world.

The inherited structures of graphic design are packaging. Useful
sometimes as containers, as presenter and protector of the message.
But they can be empty. And then they are as frames on a canvas that
has yet to be painted.

Content is the big issue in design today. The question is: what relationship does the visual language have with the verbal one? We think we
are so familiar with our own [verbal] language, it comes as a shock to
realize it is never received pure, without being coloured by the trans-
mission. We are used to seeing words as the content and then either as
text that is typeset for a layout and perhaps illustrated, or perhaps as
a script that is performed live or to a camera, again framed and illustrated in various ways. However, we are increasingly aware that these
words change in the telling; the emphasis, the context, the distractions.
And we are aware that these words cannot exist in communication
without some form of telling; thus the shaping and the shaper of that
visual/verbal language inevitably goes beyond the word or the writer.
Perhaps this changing perception is one explanation of why the
designer has been thrust up as some kind of hero of our age over the
past decade; suddenly these former crafts operatives are seen as
genius arch-manipulators that can make the world a better or worse
place. This hype obscures the fact that any designer is just part of the
whole process too, only able to add a personal contribution as an artist
may or to abnegate this contribution and simply operate as some technician in the vast message machine that goes on operating all around
us, pumping out individual and mass-communications all around us,
many thousands every day.
But some people do stand out for expressing matters
in a way that touches the many, or that first encapsulates an experience
that others have shared but not recorded. This book's subject and designer could
be put in that category. However, before looking at his work [or rather while
looking at it, here, now, simultaneously] we all have to wonder how we
are seeing, how we connect, if at all.

The writer struggles with uncertainty, then the designer struggles to
make something of this. The partnership needs to extend beyond these contributors to embrace a medium and at least one other participant. Communication
happens, if at all, by that initial emotional spark reaching across the creative
divide   firing   through   the   cerebral   cortex   and   logging   on
to...[your name here]

*the end of print, on the wall, david carson studio, san
diego, california, feb. 1995. photo: Chiharu Hayashi>>*

"DAVID CARSON IS

THE Paganini OF Typographers"

—so says Ed Fella, 1995

Carson covers. Carson's Mother Dorothy held up the font sign for *Aldus* cover

When a magazine Carson was interning on folded in 1982, money pressures led him to return to teaching. But shortly after taking up a high school post he was offered the chance to design this booming skateboarders' monthly. He did it in his spare time, after school, evenings and at weekends. It was a glorified fanzine, with up to 200 full-color pages heavily supported by advertising, and yet the editorial - copy and pictures - was largely the product of the skateboarders. "It was a great opportunity for experimentation" says the designer, who was able to respond to a readership eager for new ideas by committing himself to never doing the same thing twice without good reason. In these years he formed his approach of questioning any formal preconception.

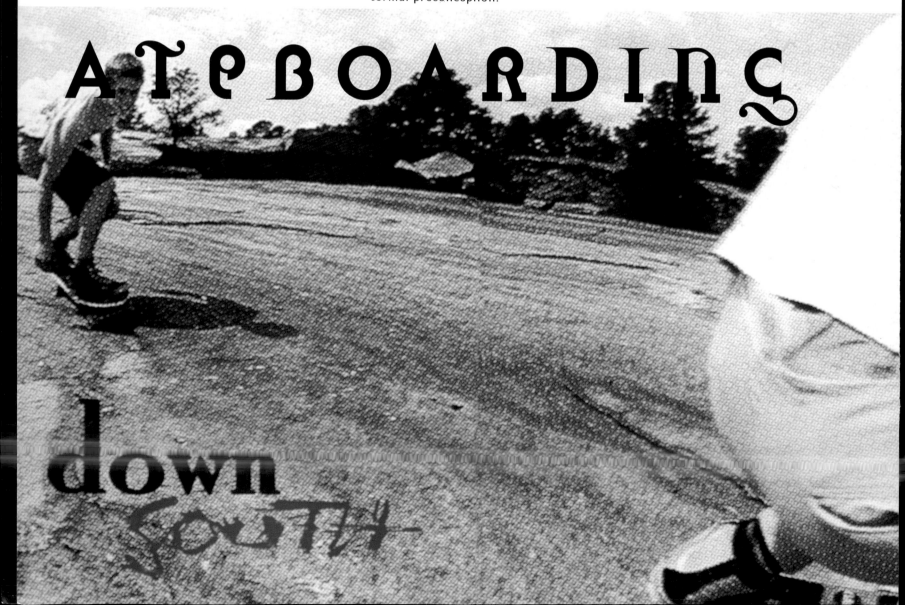

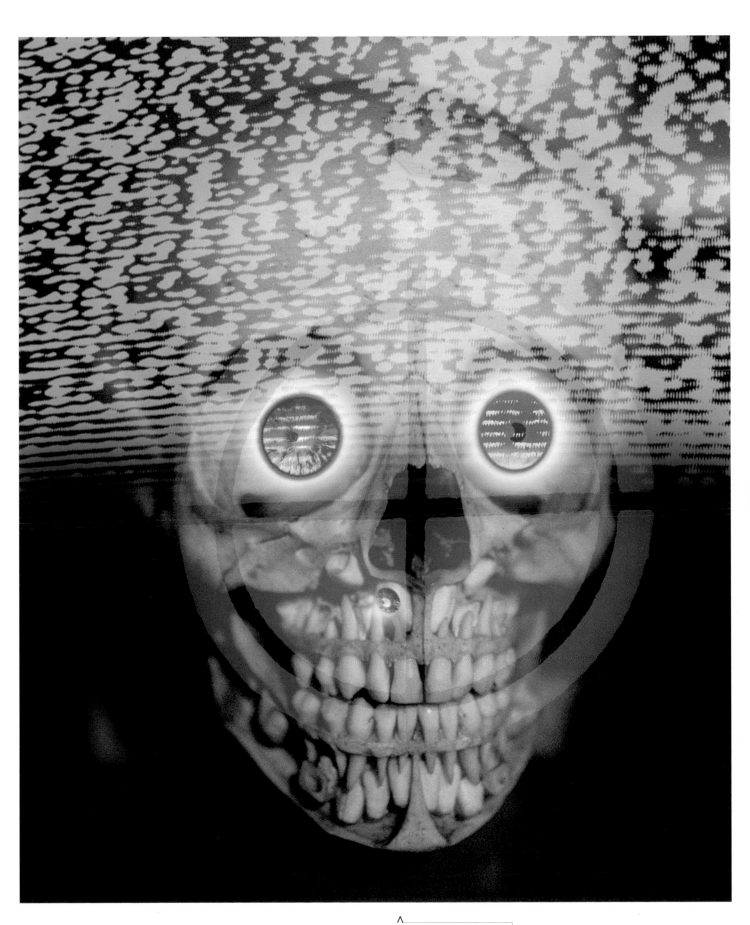

S  K

< Skateboarding in the deep south, opening spread, 1985

t a k e
a s t
a n d

s u b s c r i
b e

top l] Experiment in color acetate overlays. Photo J. Grant Brittain

top r] Subscription page, 1986. Photo J. Grant Brittain. Acetate overlays

bottom l] Subscription advertisement, 1986. Bauhaus type photocopied from a book and pasted down

bottom r] Wheel company advertisement, 1987. High school student photography class provided the images. Carson's concept and copy [note irony relating to speed]. Hate mail from readers who assumed the art director had set up the shoot

1

2

3

4

Photo-essay, 1986.
Early page number experimentation.
Photos [l to r] Zemnick,
Temmermand, J. Grant Brittain

Ohio, 1987.
Early experiment
with captions
as a design element.
Photos Swank

Chris Miller profile, 1986.
Photo J. Grant Brittain.
The layout uses the cut-up technique for
re-arranging the image, an idea
picked up from a workshop with Hans-
Rudolf Lutz. The photograph is cut,
turned face down, moved around and
then re-assembled strictly following the
random pattern. [The technique
draws on William Burroughs' writing
experiments]

Cover, 1987
Pre-computer, Carson specified
different type treatments from the
typesetter for use in paste-up,
here using not one but a section of the
whole sheet. This anticipates
the freedom that desktop computing
would provide
Photos J. Grant Brittain

Photo-essay, 1986.
Early page number experimentation.
Photos [l to r] Zemnick,
Temmermand, J. Grant Brittain

TRANSWORLD SKATEBOARDING

pro spot light **staab**

e l i n

NOBODIES
by Garry DAVIS

No one is really a nobody. No matter how insignificant one may think he is, he's somebody. From his smallest fingernail to his left ankle to his longest nose hair, he's all there. Just because ones' accomplishments have never been acknowledged by his peers should he feel discouraged. With hope, maybe he will pursue an interest for his own gain, not necessarily recognition.

Each of us have (*has*) in us an urge. Whether it is carried out through cooking, smoking, hockey, or any other thing, fulfilling these urges through action is what can transform the self-appointed "nobody" into a self-realized somebody. Illustration: There are a group of photos on the adjoining pages of a few young people who have found skateboarding. To them, it is a ticket to motivation, action, a feeling of accomplishment, fun. But when all is said and done, maybe they save the ticket stub, or maybe they don't.

P. SWANK   ALANTA   ≥ ?

P. SWANK

top] Cover, 1987. First time without cover lines. Four-color black and white. Photo J. Grant Brittain

middle] Kevin Staab profile, 1985. Original photo included skateboarder. Photo J. Grant Brittain

bottom] Article on skateboarders who are not famous, 1986. Used photo with head missing and photographer's question mark on subject identity. Text showing editor's corrections was used as artwork. Photo Todd Swank

right] Contents page, 1987. Carson has always avoided formatting contents pages, preferring to use type and image in a free, expressive manner

Content

April 1987

Volume 5

Number 2

Contents Mike McGill has developed the ollie to its near-maximum stage. A home-state (Florida) sidekick (Gelfand) move launched in fine form at the Perfect Ramp in Mesa Arizona. Photo: Grant Brittain

FEATURES

40 What About Contests? by Garry Davis and Britt Parrott

Desert Rats by Grant Brittain

72 Still Life

Pro Spotlight—Chris Miller by Neil Blender

DEPARTMENTS

92 Transmissions

94 Ramp Locals by Lance Mountain

96 Aggro Zone by Neil Blender

98 Street Sheet by Garry Davis

103 Trick Tips
Backside Curb Boneless
Ollie to Pogo
Rocket Invert
Good Buddy

104 Training Tips by Barry Zaritzky

Transaxle

106 Check Out
Ross Goodman
Gunter Mokulys
Troy Chason
Mike Crescn

110 Snow Life

123 Transinfo

146 Transpirations

Cover: Chris Cook drifting along a temporary wall during a streetstyle event in Tempe, Arizona Photo: Tod Swank

5

through the glass darkly

"I made a decision when I was very young to avoid any kind of promotion of myself within the media. Because I sat and watched, when I was a kid of 17, this lunacy going on around me, and I saw how skin-deep the whole thing was, how one could be very up one minute and extremely out the next. And one of the things responsible for that was the media. They'd set you up to knock you down. They love to love you when you're successful, and then it's boring to write about you being wonderful anymore so they steam in and rip you to pieces. I decided to avoid the whole issue as much as I could. I'd just go with what I was doing. And that seemed to work quite well, because my career has lasted quite a long time and it seems the media treat me with a degree of respect."

Glyn Johns sits back on the couch of a friend's Manhattan townhouse. His relatively low profile may have helped extend his career as a record-maker, but surely it annoys him that he has often been denied full credit for popular albums that he ghost-produced? "Didn't bother me in the least," he insists. "It wasn't why I was doing it. In the early days, when I made it as an engineer, the role of producer was somewhat different anyway, and it was difficult to become one. They were almost all in-house. And so we accepted the fact that most producers, when I started, were complete idiots. One got used to doing their work. And listen, I profited from it very well. A lot

by bill flanagan

the first time

Glyn Johns, 1988.
Musician feature on a reclusive top producer who was behind the scenes for groups such as the Rolling Stones. An appropriately murky, almost lost image was retrieved from the wastebasket

Transworld Snowboarding, 1987.
Carson did the three launch issues. He was asked to give a more conservative style and told he needed to appeal to an older audience [mistakenly]. He responded with a simple, clean treatment

Beach
Culture
1989-91

Beach Culture 1989-91

Beach what? For some, the title was an oxymoron. In reality, the magazine was one of the most innovative of all time, if the 150 or so design awards are anything to go by, along with the radical mix of editorial subject matter that drew fanatical supporters but left many (including advertisers) confused, if not downright angry. Initially, Carson was brought in on a freelance project to art direct Surfer magazine's annual publication Surfer Style, which was little more than a shopping catalogue of clothing ads supported by advertorial. However, the editor Neil Feineman and Carson had different ideas: they changed the name, the content and the frequency and managed to launch Beach Culture on a pre-recession wave of goodwill. It didn't last: the magazine got poorer by the issue, struggling along for six issues over two years before finally closing. Throughout this, though, Feineman pioneered an innovative mix of good writing on the alternative culture, using the surf scene origins as a metaphor rather than a strict template for editorial. Such freedom and inspiration was the stimulation for Carson to explore further the potential of print communication, targeting a similarly questing readership. They were out there, but they had to work hard to find the magazine, given the publisher's interest in serving the more traditional readers and advertisers. Carson was, incidentally, not oblivious to the financial straits of the magazine. "I was absolutely broke. I couldn't afford to run a car," he says, which is almost the equivalent of a white southern Californian having his legs removed. "I used to catch the train to the Beach Culture office and then walk for more than half an hour to get there."

cover photo by anton corbijn, 1990 this page: reverse wedge by ron romanosky

harry

connick

jr.

words by patrick o'donnell

⑤

conten
fall
t

In order of their appearance:
Letters
Court
Henry   Rollins
Bob   Mould
Phrancis
Brad Gerlach's brand of animal magnetism
Santa   Barbara
Texas   the   Hard   Way
Wedge   People
Uncovered: The Bathing Suit
Nature's Vortex via Henrik Drescher
                        Air
                      Winter
Portfolio: Still
            Anton   Corbijn
Zen and the art of surfboard shaping
Altitude   and   Attitude
Because there's more to snowboarding
O h i p u
The   Malibu   Fandango
As seen through the eyes of a favorite
B   o   r   n
The   Birth   of   Worldbeat
            by   Carlos   Santana
John   Doe
Dumping   Ground
Mystery   Guest
John   Hiatt
Poi   Dog   Pondering
Mazzy   Star
Mick   Jones
Phone raps with Shawn Stüssy
The   Blue   Aeroplanes
The   End   of   Summer
        and the end of this issue

^
Sixth and final issue
cover, 1991. Photo
cover, 1991. Photo Matt
cover, 1991. Mahurin

<Harry Connick Jr. profile,
1990.
Originally the tape across
    the face indicated
    where the image
    should be cropped, but
    it gave the image a
    structure that
    prompted Carson to
    include it fully

<Contents   page,   1990.
Fall issue is reflected by
falling into the page. First
use of forced justification.
Photo Ron Romanosky

Lyle Lovett/Sinead O'Connor >
    feature, 1990.
    [Out-take Polaroid
    Alan Messer.]
    Shows Lovett standing
    on position tape:
    "I felt this showed more
    about Lyle Lovett than some
    of the shots where you saw
    his face and guitar... stance,
    clothing, boots, said it all."
    Noisy type

at's all thi s no ise a b o u t anyway? wha

all this_noise a b o u t

HAT'S ALL THIS NOISE ABOUT ANYwAY? b o u t anyway?

lyle lovett photo by al an messer

the beach. A wild kaleidoscope of shimmering sand, shifting, multicolored crowds, glittering ocean and bronzed skin: An explosive cauldron of activity and ideas that keeps the rest of the world spellbound. It's where e v e r y one wants to be, but few actually are. Even fewer belong. You think you already know about beach cool—but you'd better out just to be sure.

ocean cool

a view from
the tenth
p o l e

the wedg
people

terry wong

Body surfing
at Newport Beach,
California, feature,
1991.
1991. Uses simpler
typefaces in
expressive
treatment. Note E
in "wedge"
shifts to
shifts to "people"
Photo Ron Romanosky

"EEEOOOO! WedgeWear Wedge Report, Fourth of July, and the fire-
works are flying. It's blistering hot outside already, if you can believe
that. 'Fantasies', by my band in the background. We're fantasizing big
waves, but what we have is a pulsing southwest at two-to-three—
should be fun time. Volleyball, frisbee, badminton...we can do it all. If
there's any parties let me know. I'll leave it on the afternoon message,
and I'll see you at Wedge. Allriieeggghhht!"
—Mel's WedgeWear Wedge Report, July 4, 1990
"When it's small, you get hurt. When it's big, you drown."
—Robert O: Renowned for riding "Odie," a dragon-shaped inflatable
pool toy in 8-foot Wedge.   Wedge only fires on a south-southwest
swell. That means summer. That
means crowds. The Freak Show.
Clueless, sunburned inlanders

clog the lineup—with absolutely
no concept how powerful the
waves really are. Backs and
necks can be snapped like rotten
kindling, slammed on the sand
tarmac. Sandscrapes abound, as
do noses ground down to the
cartilage. Rips drag you into the
jetties for a meat-grinder effect.
And people crowd like freeway
gawkers to catch a glimpse of
the carnage.   Riding Wedge is
like strapping yourself to an av-

concept +   p h o t o s :   ron ro m anosky
words   steve
                                   barilotti

Beach Cool opener, 1990. Background art Masanori Mishiola/K. Kenyon

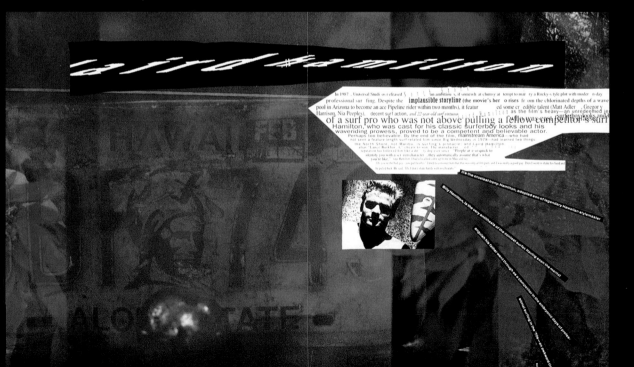

laird Hamilton

Laird Hamilton
profile, 1990.
Hawaiian flowers
and licence
plate relate to
subject's
origins;
a printer
~~error~~
inspired the
typographic
approach.
Traditional
paste-up.
Photos Art Brewer,
Jeff Girard

B o b
m O
u l d

Bob [Mould], co-founder of the legendary Minneapolis group Hüsker Du, talked to us about his life and his second solo album, *Black Sheets of Rain*, from his new apartment in New York, New York. We thought the move itself was a good place to begin: [B.C.]: Why did you move from Minnesota to New York? [Mould]: I wanted to close the book on my past. After the *Workbook* album, I went through a very strange period of upheaval in my life and changed not just musical directions but, as it turned out, a lot of friends too. While I liked Minneapolis' small-town feeling and lack of competition, I'm 29, and I'd lived there for 11 years and felt hemmed in. I didn't feel I could move beyond Hüsker Du or the insulting expectations people had of me there, so I had to leave. [B.C.]: How do you like Manhattan so far? [Mould]: I like it because it only cares about what you're doing now, not about what you've done. It's competitive and anonymous,

MORE IN BACK

ORIGINAL SPECIES

B **jo hn** kovich

john doe

Meet John Doe. It's not just the name of a new album, but a great excuse to drive into Hollywood on a day hot enough to melt even a meter maid.

Though the city is literally in flames, John Doe turns out to be the picture of cool. Maybe it's the metal bracelets on his arm; the idea that once the interview is over, he'll be on the highway, heading for the remote ranch several hours north of the city that he now calls home; or the air–conditioning. In any event, he's ready to do the day's version of the Hollywood shuffle.

Although a Los Angeles reporter recently took issue with Doe's pursuit of what the journalist called a "conventional solo career," it turns out that commercial success was a goal of X from the beginning. "Even though people don't associate X with that, it was always important to all of us to be successful," he says. "We always made the best records, gave the best performances and struck the best business deals we could. The only thing we didn't do was make inane music and bend over backwards in terms of making c o n c e s s i o n s ."

Surprisingly, Doe recalls that back in the late seventies, he, Exene and fellow punkers like Top Jimmy would sit around at night "talking about making a lot of money and getting the fuck out of L.A. We knew money would give us the freedom to do things we wanted, like living in the country. We didn't see anything wrong with providing a service and getting paid what we deserved for that."

Although they themselves ultimately didn't make lots of money from X, the band was successful. "We sold 150,000 copies an album and stood for the right things. We had good ideals. Those don't change unless you're tempted and make concessions a little at a time."

ofeverything,butits effectdependsent irely uponourcom- pliance. Todepart fromthecollec- tivemindistoenter aninteresting con- flict.

Skateboarding has for decades- survivedthescour- geof p u b l i c d i staste. More- thananalternati v e, itseemssubver- sivetothestability ourcultureaspires to.Seemsisitselfa subversiveword. Skateboarding- was created as a new approach to a common environment. Throughitsown evolution,newercustom arenas were both de-

merce, o f con- sumer conven- ience. A sindividu- almembers, ourimmediateexpe r i e n c e i s t h e p a v e d legacyofourancestry.Andtheresourceswe i

Face feature, 1990.
Explores crop point in the image.
Photo Art Brewer

Travel article on Texas, 1991.
Rainy day VW van window.
Photo Pat Blashill

Global warming
        feature, 1990.
Illustration Lane
        Smith

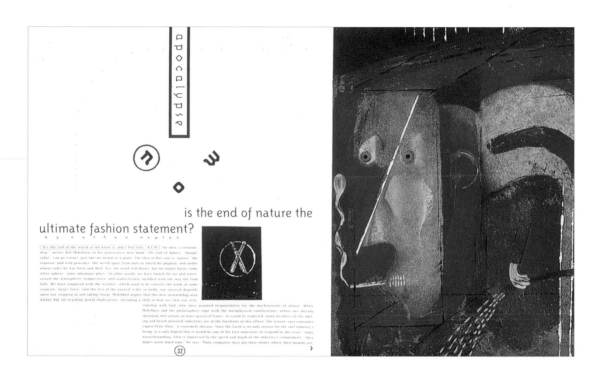

Blind surfer feature,
        1991.
Report on a person
        who teaches
        blind people
        to surf: this
        opener turns
        to an unspecified
        point later in the
        magazine where
        the article ran

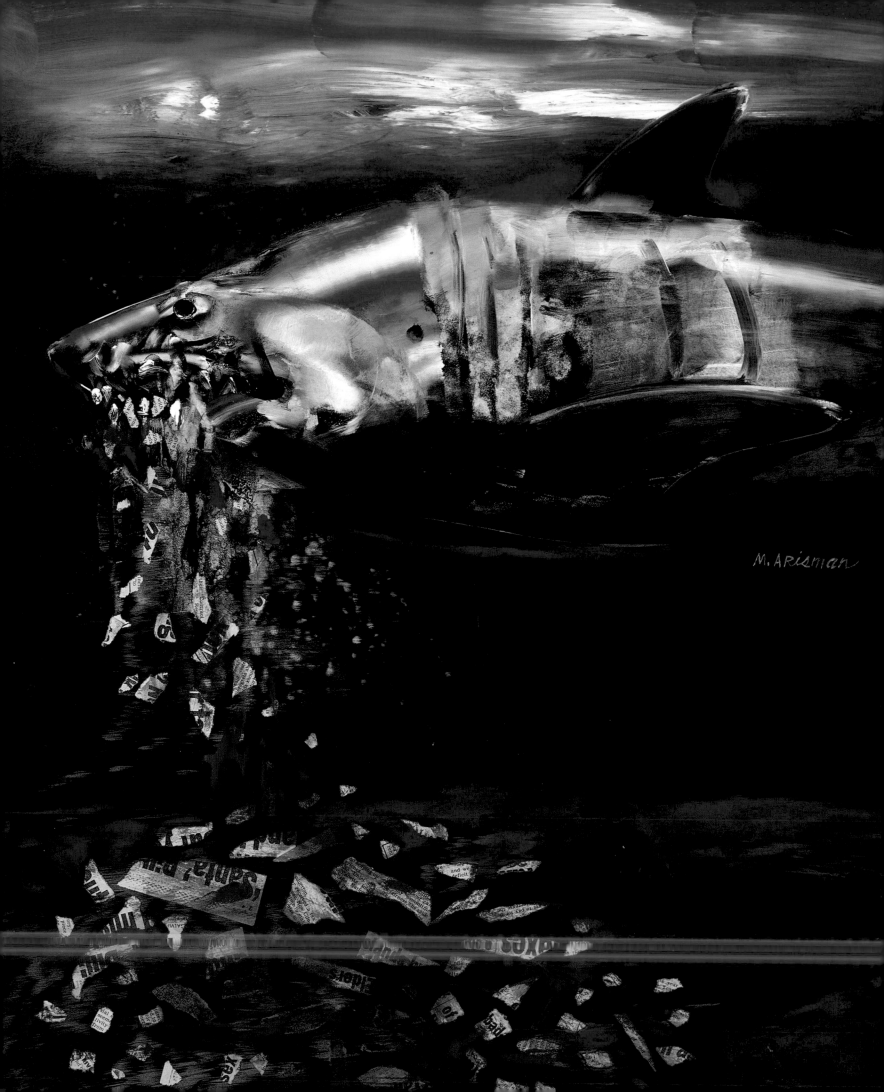

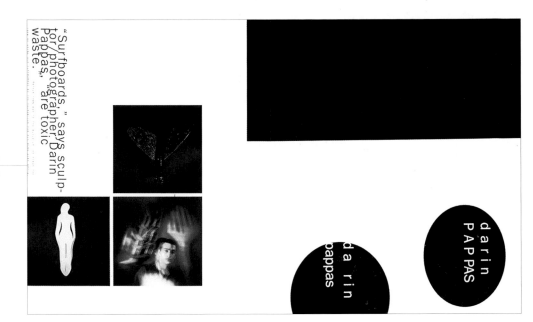

Sculptor profile, 1991.

Explores strong abstract shapes.

"Surfboards," says sculptor/photographer Darin Pappas, "are toxic waste."

darin PAPPAS

darin pappas

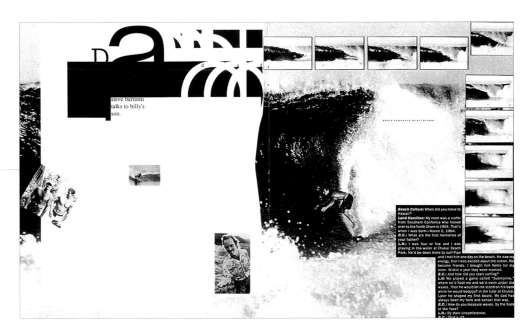

Dad, 1991.

Photo sequence by Art Brewer.

steve bartiotti talks to billy's son.

photo sequence by art brewer

Beach Culture: When did you move to Hawaii?
Laird Hamilton: My mom was a surfer from Southern California who moved over to the North Shore in 1964. That's when I was born—March 2, 1964.
B.C.: What are the first memories of your father?
L.H.: I was four or five and I was playing in the water at Ehukai Beach Park. He'd be down there to surf Pipe and I met him one day on the beach. He saw my energy, that I was excited about the ocean. We became friends. I brought him home for my mom. Within a year they were married.
B.C.: And how did you start surfing?
L.H.: We played a game called "Submarine," where he'd hold me and we'd swim under the waves. Then he would let me stand on his back while he would bodysurf in the tube at Ehukai. Later he shaped my first board. My dad has always been my hero and sensei that way.
B.C.: How do you measure waves, by the back or the face?
L.H.: By their circumference.

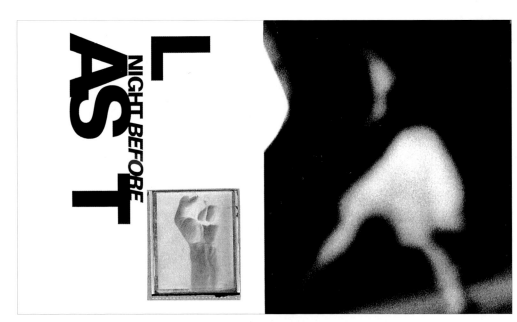

< THE END OF PRINT [marshall arisman

Feature on Russian ballet performance contrasted with Public Enemy rap concert, 1991.

Photo Steve Sherman

LAST NIGHT BEFORE

Swimsuit history, 1990.
Severe crop and montage.
Photo Art Brewer

M. Arisman

Graceland tour feature,
1991. Photo of Jetstream
trailer by Alan Lebudde

E LAND,
GRACE
PARA
LAND, PARA
DISE G
DISE G
ARDEN, AND
ST. COCA
COLA

BEACH CULT u 9 0 re

The End of Summer

Bob Mould
Singing In the Rain

Anton Corbijn:
The Man Who Shot U–2

Brad Gerlach
Animal Magnetism

Mick Jones
On Apocalypse Beach

Special No-Emigre-Fonts
Issue

Punk Gods; Soul Surfers:
John Doe
Henry Rollins
Iggy Pop
Phranc
John Hiatt

Mazzy Star
Rising

Bathing Suits
Yesterday and Today

Wedge People

The Shred–
Where Attitude Meets
Altitude

Robert Ferrigno
Turned On

Henrik Drescher
Waste Deep

Road Tripping:
Baja
Austin
Santa Barbara
Diamond Head

VOL 1#4 OCT/NOV $2.95

01552 10

Cover four, 1990. Photo Anton Corbijn [his early colour work]

T O N Y

People

rarely give Tony Hawk the credit he deserves. I'm not talking of the general applause or adulation he gets from being in his position, but the understanding of just what it takes to be in his shoes. Of the subtext behind his continual achievements, staying on the very top seat after year knowing that everyone is waiting for him to fail. ■ Although that pressure can be unbelievable, I have only seen it get to him once. It was at the end of one during the Vision NSA finals. He had come off an incredible two year winning streak, but seemed particularly pensive. He said he was getting tired of it, and decided he didn't want to compete anymore. The other skaters were frustrated by his complete domination and had settled for battling it out for second place. On his final run of the contest he fell, causing him to blow a safe lead. ■ I vividly remember watching him, thinking that he looked almost happy, kind of relieved. He got up from the bottom of the ramp, took off his helmet, waved to the crowd of screaming skaters and humbly walked out of sight. To witness Tony falling during a contest is about as rare as a good six foot swell hitting the Wedge. Since he despises not doing his best and ended up coming in fourth. I believe he threw that contest—not consciously, but because he needed to break that edge. ■ After that, he took a break. When he came back, he was transformed, jumping right back into the competitive scene with an intensity and sureness of himself that few only gets after years of dedicated effort. ■ He still dominates the vertical competitions, but now is even working streetstyle contests, which he barely qualified for several years ago. ■ It's not just the contests either. I recently went to him and asked that he show me all his latest tricks and variations. He showed me maneuvers I just only had never seen but also thought impossible. ■ Afterwards, as a joke, I asked him if that was all. There's a few I'm playing with in my head, he said. I turned the camera back on. Then without taking more than three tries with each one, he worked out four of the most avant garde, complicated moves I'd ever seen. His friends who were there couldn't believe what they had just seen. Though Tony seemed very much at ease inwardly, you could tell he was quite happy. ■ He should be. After all these years, he still is not just inventing tricks but developing a new style, movement, and direction for all other skaters to follow.

W O R D S B Y H A Y E S H E N D E R S O N

I L L U S T R A T I O N S T A C Y P E R A L T A

h a w k

1. Squeeze clutch levers together, which opens clutch jaws. Insert pencil as far as it will go.

Eugene, Oregon,
1992. Photo DC

opposite]
Empty storefront,
New Zealand, 1993

SURFER STYLE'S

$3.9

Spring

BEACH CULT URE

Report on a boy dying of cancer, 1991.

Illustration Paul Davis

The man with the shaved head and surfboards didn't notice that the ocean water was unseasonably warm for California in late October. He just tended to a box that was balanced on one of the boards like it was more precious than gold. The box had a red piece of cloth tied to it. The man slowly paddled the boards away from the shore avoiding the beach break until he was way past the lineup. He kept paddling. When he had almost vanished, he pushed the board with the box on it out to sea. The man with no hair waved a small goodbye. He had lost a son.

The boy's name was Hunter, as if someone knew in advance that he would need to be brave. At age three, his bone marrow started producing too many white blood cells, crowding out the life-giving red blood cells. The kick in his step went quickly. Then, when the chemo made his hair fall out, Hunter's dad shaved his head to show Hunter there was nothing to fear.

In the ward, the kid in the next bed had a Superman doll. It was the first Superman Hunter had ever seen. After the kid left the ward, a nurse brought Hunter a Superman doll of his own. Soon Hunter had his own pair of Superman pajamas.

They say he was quite an inspiration, walking down the halls of the ward in his Superman p's, pushing the pole that carried the I.V. bottles that fed his diabetics to his cancerous body. On the rare visits home, he sometimes wore his Superman costume to the party. When the other little kids gathered around, he told them, "I'm not really Superman. This is just an outfit."

By the time Hunter turned four, the white blood cells had consumed his little body. His imaginary dog, Lilly, was always by his side to play and to pretend with. His mother told him that things were getting better, but Hunter knew different. He had the wisdom, even at age four, that comes to anyone who is terminally ill. One day he announced that Lilly had died. He would have to go to heaven to feed her.

In his last days, Hunter went home under a hospice program. People tried to encourage him, but he mustered facile answers. "I know I will never feel better again." On Friday, he stopped eating. Saturday, he stopped drinking. That night he died in his mom's arms. His last word was a little moan.

After he died they changed him into his Superman outfit, as if it was his last wish. His parents had cried for eight months through his ordeal, but they cried that night like never before. Hunter was gone. By the time the mortician arrived, his body was already stiff. Hunter didn't live there anymore.

They cremated Hunter in his Superman outfit. His dad and a friend placed his urn on a surfboard and paddled it far out into the ocean. They tied his red cape around the urn.

At the service they played Hunter's favorite song, "There's a hole in my bucket." Goofy sang the original. We heard the whole thing. Someone said Hunter knew almost every word of it. By the time Goofy sang the last verse, we could all feel the hole.

In an odd way, no one was angry that Hunter had gone. They were only grateful that God had brought Hunter into their lives.

Just the room was filled with so much genuine love and care was curious. Hunter had never achieved anything significant by worldly standards; he hadn't received a college diploma, didn't discover any cures, was never a financial success. Yet his value as a human being was immeasurable. He didn't have to accomplish anything to be loved or missed. Just being himself was enough to break the hearts of the world around him.

The morning of the service someone stopped at a supermarket to pick up a special cake they had ordered from the bakery. At the checkout line, a young couple peeked into the cake box and saw the Superman "S."

"Oh, how cute, a birthday cake," they said. "No," the friend said, it's not a birthday, it was a cake for a four-year-old boy's funeral. Just above the "S," the icing read, "GOODBYE, SUPERMAN." ✕

words: & david murie   illustration: paul davis

---

can a visionary be from the mid-west

and other relevant musings on the beach

If you ask me, so much of this (surf) industry is based upon the notions of hip insiders: It's "our beach," "Our lifestyle." Wear the correct thing; surf the correct breaks; have the correct friends, plan a very-correct foreign surf trip extravaganza.

Some insiders won't even admit they're from the Mid-west. And this is the problem. "Surfing" used to be about the force of gravity upon human minds, bodies and water. Now it's about peer pressure and proximity of birthplace to pointbreak. Puh-lease.

Because the real beach is in the mind. In fact, anything of value is in there, including your first kiss and for that matter, your next. For me the smell of coconut and the sound of that song "Beach Baby" are "at the beach" in my mind.

My Beach is really a group of beaches tucked away in the Protestant Florida resort town of Naples. In the Seventies, Naples had the dubious honor of boasting more Rolls-Royces, alcoholics, golf courses and millionaires per capita than any other U.S. town. We also were blessed seasonally with representatives of two major South Florida professions: retiree and migrant worker.

profession: developer/realtor. I often wonder if he knew the impact his employer had upon the wetlands. Back then, when it rained we could skimboard for days in the puddles. These days, marks in the trees tell of seasonal fires.

Back then, our moms all looked like moms on The Wonder Years. Once mine took me and my sister to the beach with our pet duck, Cheeper. He was an Easter duck, and, we thought, a boy

duck. Then he laid an egg. Oh well.

I can still remember our duck-like march to the water: Mom, me, Faith and, in the rear, Cheeper. I can still see Cheeper bobbing up and down like a rubber duck on the waves.

We lived inland, seven miles. How uncool that was. Most of my earliest beach memories include waking up early on weekends or during the summer so Mom could drop me and a girlfriend off on her way to work.

We had to stay all day, but that was okay because back then, you could never be too tan. Plus, it took all the attention away from your zits. My mom, a fair-skinned redhead, always told me to wear a hat or put a towel over my face, but that just made me more determined to burn. Once, I got sent home from high school because my English teacher couldn't look at my sunburn without wincing. The doctor made me put this brown stuff that looked like apple butter on my face for two days. So many other memories. Like the time in ninth

by Hope Winsborough

Non-coastal cool, 1991.

Illustration Milton Glaser

Real Life in the Coastal Zone

b**each**y

Billy Gould doesn't hang out at the beach More, and has been on the road for two has just moved to Ocean Beach so he "My beach is intimate and make friends with it. They saw my ocean grow up around the lifestyle. last January. We went surfing, and it so white you needed sunglasses to look I fell off the cliff while staring at the mount a surfboard rack on my motorcycle beaches and lack of crowds. Street. My first surf came some 15 Southern California days past. Sand. trips. Friends visiting from up north, Wish I still had it. near coastal smells, so I moved to Ocean Golden Gate Bridge for surf checks. morning and late-day bike rides with my along the streets in the Sunset district. our music and stage ways, but hairspray spontaneity. It's kind of like when you that. You work around the moods, carve

as much as he would like to, but it's not for years. Currently in San Francisco putting a can catch up on his life and enjoy "his" tight, like the band. My parents introduced feelings as healthy rather than self- "Because of that, everywhere I was unreal. A green, tropical jungle, all at it. The surf was happening and warm. Or perfect waves. Everyone laughed at me then, and head south. I like Mexico, and used to go "That was the way it used to be years ago; and my memories of it are like Surf. Sun. Those chubascos pumping swell wailed by sneaker sets. It was cool. My first "Now, after being on tour for two Beach—two blocks to the sand. I often find Mostly I just hang around Ocean Beach, lady, time tripping along the strand or on my "It's no different with our music. and Spandex are not our style. When the five go surfing. The conditions change constantly. off the attitudes and pull into ideas. It's tight

lack of trying. He's in a band called Faith No record together with the rest of the band, he me to my first beach, and encouraged me to destructive so I've been lucky enough to go is "my beach." Like down at Rock In Rio tangled and jutting down onto bleached sand like the time on Maui and Honolua Bay when "Who knows? Maybe someday I'll all the time. Maybe it's because of the great where I grew up in Del Mar, around 19th Polaroids. Quick, click remembrances of lines onto the coast; or Black's Beach cliff board was a plastic fantastic 6'4" swallow. years, I'm city-bummed. I had to get back myself radar-aimed at Fort Point under the which is my beach now. I love those early- black and white Italian Moto Guzzi motorcycle. We could take a more corporate approach to of us are together, there are sparks and You have to adapt and flex. The band's like and together—just like my beach." ✕

My Beach feature, 1991.
"This is gibberish" said the editor as he handed it back.
Photo Ken McKnight.

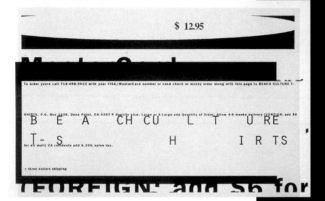

$ 12.95

To order yours call 714-496-5922 with your VISA/MasterCard number or send check or money order along with this page to BEACH CULTURE T-

SHIRTS, P.O. Box 1020, Dana Point, CA 9262 9 Specify size: Large or X-Large and Quantity of Order. Allow 4-8 weeks delivery (FOREIGN: add $6

B E A CH CU L T U RE
T - S   H   I RTS
for air mail) CA residents add 8.25% sales tax.

+ three dollars shipping

[FOREIGN: and $6 for

T-shirt ad, 1991.
An ad selling the shirt sight unseen: if
you like the look of the ad, of the magazine, you probably would like the shirt

summer's here
JUNE 19,

ture **culture**
ture

get some cultur e and check out :

two faces for the 90's— john wesley harding (singer-songwriter) , beach culture magazine.

the j e s u s and mary th e chain on the Santa Monica pier

mary;'s danish on bottled w a ter ;
plus the u s u a l mix of art, places, st Yle

and ATTItUDE. our special   on the Road in jamaica, ZANZIBAR, Hawaii and k e n t u c k y

the ULTIMATE—A sport

rd stores. TIMATE—A sport t h a t l i v e s u p to its name.
on the road in jamaica, ZANZIBAR, Hawaii and k e n t u c k y
the j e s u s and mary c h a i n on the S
anta Monica pier

bbook.stores

BESHOPS

Next issue page, 1990.
It's all there, somewhere.
Photo Art Brewer.

Contents page, 1991.

Plays with idea of information and numbers on contents pages –
this was the issue that first dropped page numbers. Generated on
computer, pasted down as overlays. Typeface Hobo; a conscious
effort to use the worst typeface at hand in an interesting way.
Photo Larry Bartholomew

Iopa Veles

hard to beat,

Contents page, issue six, 1991.
Photo Jon Foster

< Background: Face feature on
Lopa Veles. Photos Art Brewer >

Memorable quote:

"Another bummah day

men. Future plans:

Get married (off and on).

that

h at

anging

carmine st.

The year is 1979. And 1942. At a small neighborhood pool in Greenwich Village, a movie crew is time-tripping 30-odd years into the past to film "Raging Bull," the story of boxer Jake LaMotta. A gang of skinny, shirtless kids holler from a rooftop as the cameras follow Robert DeNiro (playing LaMotta). He buys a soda at the concession stand, and sits at a picnic table with the actor playing LaMotta's brother. Around the pool, women in one-piece bathing suits relax in chaise lounges, and local Mafia hoods in tropical shirts play cards. DeNiro has eyes for only one: the platinum blonde who sits at pool's edge, luxuriantly paddling her long legs in the cool water. The camera moves in for a close-up of her legs...and director Martin Scorsese calls.

Hanging At Carmine Street, feature on a New York public swimming pool, 1991. An opportunity to hang some type.
Photo Pat Blashill
[background: Mister Morrison opener

1 GRAN FABRICA DE NAIPES
DE TODOS ESTILOS

face

carl
lumbly

Carl Lumbly, seen most recently in a recurring role on LA Law, is a busy actor
whose work in movies such as the cult sensation, Buckaroo Banzai, and in
the upcoming film, Pacific Heights with Melanie Griffith,
and plays such as Eden and Gospel at Colonnus, has made him an "actor's
actor." Although he grew up in Minneapolis, he is Jamaican, and retains his
love for the beach. We caught up with him for a vegetarian lunch
of dirty rice and steamed vegetables at Café Beignet, one of his
favorite restaurants, a stone's-throw from the famed Bay Street surf break in Santa
Monica. Q. Are things better today for black actors? A. While   MORE ON 67

p h r a n c

Back in the late seventies, when I'm any good. I wish I had more
West Coast punk was in its heyday, guts—I see a big wave, want to
a diminutive performer named Phranc take it and even start to move
started the hardcore crowd with a on it. But then I chicken out.
song called "Take Off Your Swasti- It's funny to me that I do, be-
kas". More amazingly, they did. And cause I never feel safer than
began to spread the word about when I am out in the water with
Phranc, the all-American, Jewish, the ocean all around me."
lesbian folksinger.   If performing has some of
That she was also a surfer went the same risks, she has learned
largely unnoticed. But she is, and to navigate them better. "It's
has impeccable beach roots. She was scary to try out new material,
in the same third grade class as because the only test is if the
Stacy Peralta at the Mar Vista El- people respond. There have been
ementary School, hung out at Bay times I was ready to try some-
Street during the school year. And thing but backed out at the last
during the summer, she and the rest minute because I was fright-
of the family relocated to Newport ened. No one else knew about
Beach, where her grandparents lived. it, but I did. I felt like I had
"It was the part of Newport with cheated, and got no gratifica-
the white, red-neck, blond-surfer- tion from the performance."
babe mentality," she says. "I didn't   Gratification shouldn't be a
fit in, but since I was on the outside problem these days. Her first
of everything, not just the surfer album, Phranc: Folksinger,
fantasy, that was nothing new. I which she financed by giving
handled it by becoming good at one swimming lessons, is finally
swimming. Is finally swimming, like the gui- being released on CD. She com-
tar or the ocean."   pleted a video for her song, "One
Despite the isolation, she enjoyed of the Girls," which uses swim-
"perfect summers. I had a few friends, tage shots of her early swim-
and spent a lot of time bodysurfing ming and surfing days. And she's
with my mother. I took swimming working on her third album,
lessons from the Parks and Recre- which is scheduled for release
ation Department, and, when I was this winter.
nine, took surfing lessons too."   She can't wait. "With three
She learned on and still uses a albums, "she laughs, "the record
longboard. And although she's been stores have to give you your
surfing for years now. "I can't say own bin." X

EL PAJARO

LA MANO

left] Face feature; Carl Lumbly.
Photo Art Brewer

right] Phranc profile, 1990.
Color rather than space
differentiates type columns

background] Mexican surf trip, 1991.
Found letterpress type,
Mexican playing cards,
napkin from famous Baja bar

altitude and attitude

fotos : trujillo + bing + fawcett

test : doug palladini

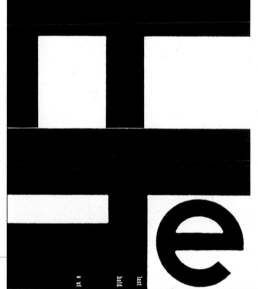

DAVID LYNCH, UNEARTHED

34

Snowboarding article, 1990.
To get the desired copy
shape, which reflects the
altitude and attitude, the article was
repeated twice.
Photos Trujillo, Bing, Fawcett

Property feature, 1991.
"The last hold out" subject is explored
in headline type, where the 1920s e is
surrounded by a new face.
Photo Steve Sherman

David Lynch profile, 1990.
Carson interprets the subtle rule-
breaking of Lynch's work by
breaking an unquestioned rule of type –
that you don't run body copy
down the gutter. The second column
runs neatly down with the staples
right through it. The black shape at the
bottom is the result of not putting
the copier lid fully down.
Photo Jan Weinberg

John Wesley Harding feature, 1990.

Preferred shot on the

contact sheet used for the page.

Photo Art Brewer

Galaxie 500 profile, 1990.

Photo Pat Blashill

Sixth issue openers, 1991.

Sixth issue openers, 1991. New direction in titles, the

shapes derived entirely from repetition

and manipulation of words, with exploration of

negative space.

negative space. Photos Steve Sherman

j o h n
w e s l
e y h a
r d i n
g

First-ever Southern California performance is just
hours away, but John Wesley
Harding looks anything but
nervous as he sits in the fad-
ing afternoon sun playing
chess. He greets the offer
to postpone the interview
for several minutes with a
broad, apologetic grin. "I'm
a bit enthralled at the moment," he says. ... W h e n
soon comes to a stopping
point, puts the magnetic
(pocket) chess set away,
and starts talking. With a
deep voice so grateful would
envy, he responds to praise
for his album, Here Comes
the Groom, with seemingly
genuine enthusiasm . . . I
t . . . is a reaction he's getting used to. Although the
record was released with
relatively little fanfare this
past spring it quickly

g a l a x i e
500

Like Raymond Carver stories, Galaxie 500 songs are simple.
They're simple and bleak, but full of detail. Claustrophobically
close yet untouchably distant. If it weren't necessary to go out
for orange juice, a new pair of jeans, an obscure Velvet Underground bootleg, or just to see how odd people look, Galaxie 500
might never venture beyond four walls. With moody, introspective
lyrics—about misunderstanding, love's failure, confusion, detach-
ment and fear—they confide; with lumbering guitar, wandering
drums and an urging bass, they transport. Singer/guitarist Dean
Wareham, a boy whose thoughts take him farther than his feet, admits, "We are very still." Wareham, bassist Naomi Yang and drum-
mer Damon Krukowski have known each other since high school,
when they lived in New York. In 1988, they fell into Galaxie 500

mer, is cleaner than *Today*, but
cleaner only in the sense that
American life in the late '80s—as
compared to the late '60s—was.
"Decomposing Trees" is sad and romantic; like a heroin haze without
the puncture. The mood lingers
through 10 songs, narrowly escap-
ing despondency with an accidental
joyful strum of the guitar. With a
rather literary use of detail, Wareham writes small songs—instead of
anthems—articulating the isolation
with which he and his generation
have become familiar. In the love
song "When Will You Come Home,"
he sings (in a voice whining like
Neil Young), "I'm crawling on all
fours, making noises like a dog,
making noises you can't hear." It's
a lyric that transcends simple disintegration of love; it's desperate expression lost in an indiffer-
ent culture. Like the best short stories and songs, Galaxie 500's music reflects an attitude in the
context of time and place. The band understands what Morrissey means when he sings, "I'm not happy

The Belly-Up Tavern, Solana Beach, California.
Owner Dave Hodges didn't envision staying in business very long, which explains the name. "We wanted people to have a fun place to
go that was entertainment-oriented, and not just for drinking." he says...

gary linden: of wine and wa...
gary L I N D E N : aving and waves

When you think of Art Deco, you might
think of your grandparents' apartment building in
Miami or, if you are so inclined, of the 1925 Paris
Exposition d'Arte Decoratif, which introduced the
style to the world. You might even think of the 1939 World's Fair.
Chances are you would not think of California.

But, says landscape architect and Deco enthusiast John
Taylor, California has made a significant albeit unheralded contribution to the movement. "When I moved to California in 1996," he
says, "I was struck by how much 20th-century architecture there
was here...

opposite, top]

Travel piece, 1991.

Illustration Gary Baseman,

photo Anthony Artiago

opposite, bottom]

Fashion spread, 1991.

Hand-lettering DC,

photo Larry Bartholomew

opposite, background]

Photo by Bradford **Walker**

Evans Hitz

appeared in the second issue

[1990

the professional surfing tour
the association of surfing professionals tour
by Derek Hynd

4

PrETTY

PICTURES FROM

EUROpe

Cover, 1990. Photo Geof Kern, originally submitted for inside article, but surprise quality and compositional strength made it the cover >

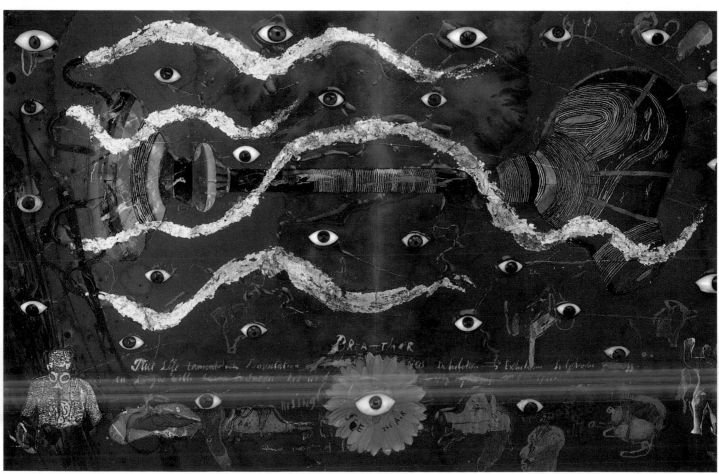

< Environmental concern, 1990.

No copy, just illustration by Henrik Drescher

BEACH CULTURE

1990

Water

david
The First Interview
lynch

sinéad
o'connor

art+music surf + skate
style+attitude

the day
manson
met the beach boy

the birth of
the endless
summer

s u m m e r

0 373429 2

VOL. 1 #3 AUG/SEPT $2.95

Surfer
1991-2

When Beach Culture folded, Carson was asked by the parent company, Surfer Publications, to look at its flagship title. The redesign gave him the opportunity to apply his radical approach to a fairly conservative magazine, stripping away the staid conventions of a 33-year-old title that was working to a 1970s design. While he struggled to get his ideas adopted at the time, it is notable that elements of his work have since been copied across the surfing press. For all the innovation of his art direction, the publishers had to accept the strength of understanding the designer had for the subject matter: his years as a top pro surfer gave him unchallengeable credentials for interpreting the subject matter.

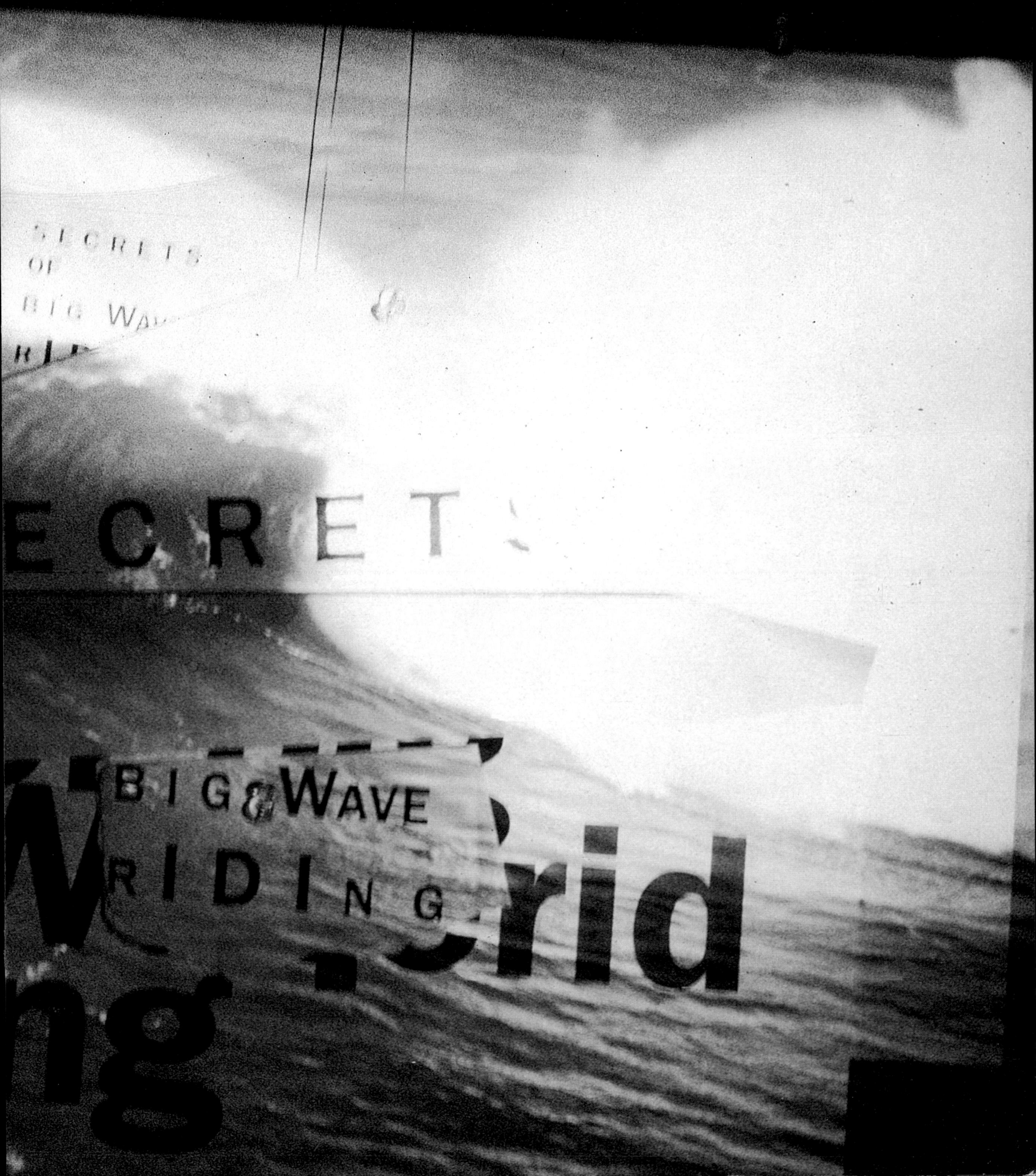
SECRETS
OF
ECRET
BIG & WAVE
RIDING
rid
ng

SURFER

Poster INSIDE

**KRAKATOA:DREAM
WAVES AND DISASTER.
JEFF BOOTH IS NOT A
JERK.WETSUIT BUYER'S
GUIDE.WELCOME TO
WEASEL REEF-NOT!**

Photo Bob Barbour >

< previous spread]   Secrets of big wave riding, 1992.

Image projected on wood, type taped on top, re-photographed.

Photo Art Brewer

Backgrounds Joseph Polevey

Big Time, 1992. Colour photo converted to black and white to make the waves more unfriendly

BIG TIME

YEARS of preparation. MONTHS of waiting. DAYS of search. HOURS until sunrise. MINUTES of terror. SECONDS of glory. BIG is here.

tony moniz. photo: t. tsuchiya.

Surfing In Japan, 1992. Early use of Photoshop for type manipulation

If you've been there, you know Japan has great surf, plenty of stoked and friendly locals, and a booming surf industry. But changes are you've never been there. Few American surfers have. It's too far, we say. Too expensive. Too foreign. Now you know what you've been missing.

JAPAN

KAIFU, ON THE ISLAND OF SHIKOKU, IS CONSIDERED THE NORTH SHORE OF JAPAN. IT'S A SURF CENTER POPULATED BY SHAPERS, GLASSERS AND OTHER CRAFTSMEN WHO MOVE THERE FROM ALL OVER JAPAN TO ENJOY THE WAVES, THE NATURAL BEAUTY AND THE CAMARADERIE OF OTHER SURFERS. THE MAIN SURF SPOT IS THE SANDBAR AT THE MOUTH OF THE KAIFU RIVER. PHOTO: KIN.

If you turned to this page expecting T&A, read on and learn why

SEXISM SUCKS

by Matt Warshaw

Consider the durability of the word "chick." The Beats invented the expression about 40 years ago; it got a push from the counterculture, easily survived early '70s feminism, and now stands as arguably the English-speaking world's most popular slang word for girl or woman. In surfing, virtually no other description for female exists.

As demonstrated by reigning ASP men's world champion Damien Hardman, after watching a women's heat last year, usage is as follows: "That's the best I've ever seen a chick surf."

An article on sexism in surfing, therefore,

might begin with a quick lesson in semantics: "Chick" is derogatory, in the same category as "hebe," "nigger" and "faggot." The fact that a world champion can nonchalantly describe a peer as "chick" in an interview, without recrimination, only hints at the length, breadth and depth of sexism in surfing. Surfing's gender morals, in a word, suck. Hardman is champ; ignorance is king.

58
SURFER Magazine

illustration by anita kunz

pro fi le

j
manners
AND J
image

Jeff Booth has a lot going on between the legs of the ASP World Tour. He left Australia rated eighth in the world,

BY BEN MARCUS

stopped by Tavarua for a couple days, then came home to Laguna Beach to move into a new house. Booth's pad is older, comfortable with three bedrooms, a big yard and a garage full of surfboards. The three hundred thousand bucks Booth signed for may be low end for Laguna Beach real

boo th

the photos that changed the way we surf

surf

by matt george

Photos That Changed the Way We Surf, 1992. Early version of Barry Deck's Template Gothic, one of the most influential typefaces of the early 1990s, features in this spread from first issue of the redesigned Surfer

art
brewer

portf
olio

photo by matt mahurin

Portfolio of Art Brewer, 1992. Photo Matt Mahurin, featuring illustration on photography. Name/headline plays off treatment photographers usually get for their name credit

COLD
SWEAT

a big-wave secret spot for
30 years, northern california's
maverick's emerges from
the mist.

Cold Sweat, 1992.
Letterpress type helps
evoke unfriendly
environment of a
dangerous surfing
area. Photo Don
Montgomery

Ray Gun 1992-

Marvin Jarrett, former publisher of Creem, would be the music and fashion magazine of tive, but now conservative, music press. Ray Gun (a name that alludes to a line in a to the artist Claes Oldenburg's proposed early 1960s). Initially Jarrett recruited the Neil Feineman, although Feineman left after has not entirely delivered a new music and in its art direction it has carried revolution layout, his art direction has opened the way tors and photographers, as well as provid content area is Sound In Print, where six to readers' illustrations of song lyrics; in this art magazine, along with its music scene *content* challenges the notion of design as words and pictures. How Ray Gun looks is content. The magazine grew rapidly to a cir tional distribution.

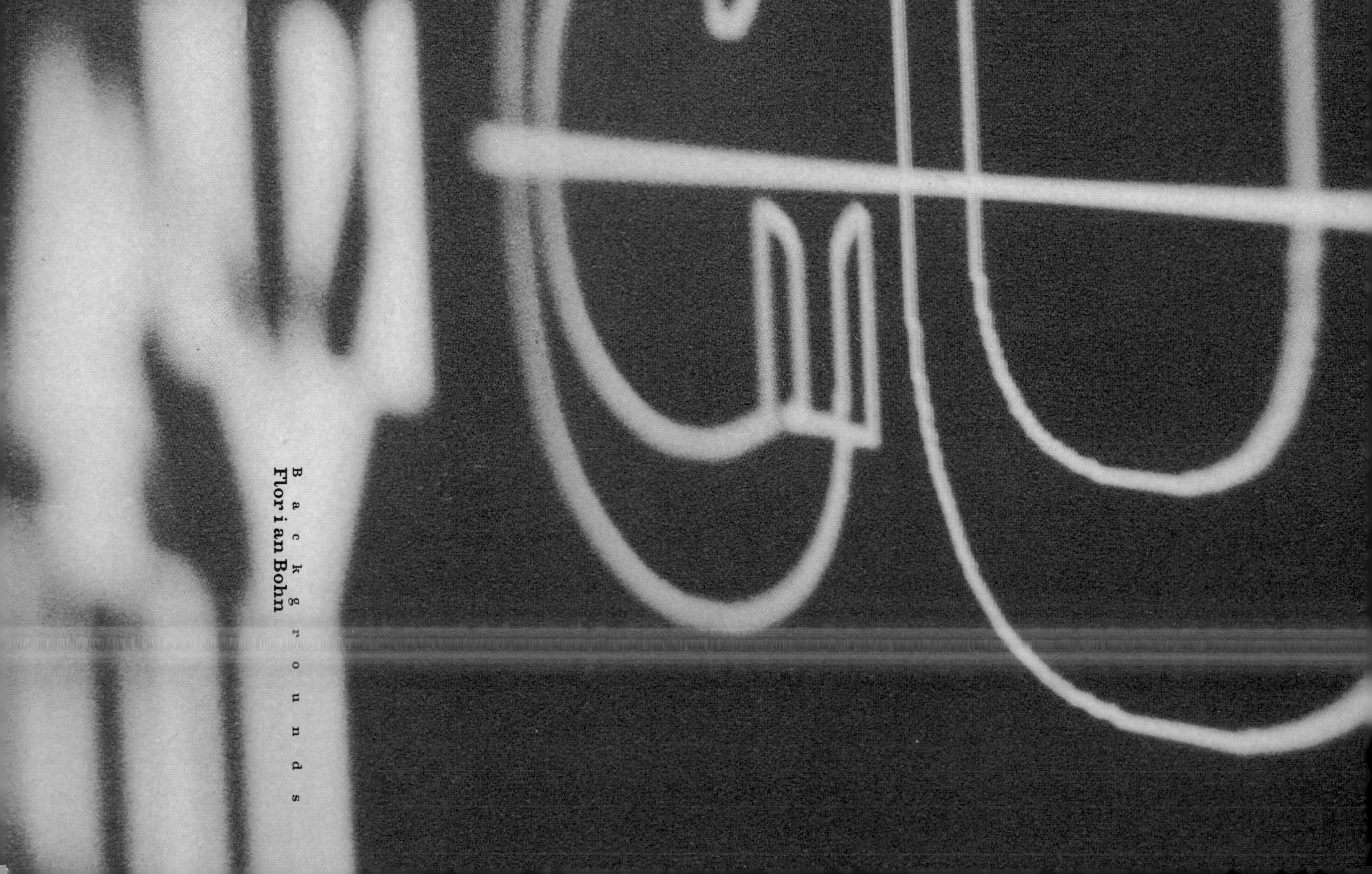

Backgrounds

Florian Bohn

conceived the idea of a new magazine that
the 1990s, a challenge to the once alterna-
From a base in Los Angeles, he launched
David Bowie song and, inadvertently, links
renaming/reshaping of New York in the
Beach Culture team of Carson and editor
a handful of issues. The monthly magazine
style agenda through the written word, but
ary content: besides Carson's own ideas in
for unusually free work by major illustra-
ing a platform for new talents. One radical
eight pages each issue are given over to
manner, Ray Gun exists as a popular fine
coverage. The strength of *art direction as*
mere form, as a container for the content of
not a style: it is the heart of the magazine's
culation of more than 120,000, with interna-

Inspiral Carpets, 1992.
Hand-carved letters were
used to print name.
    Laser print output was
    pasted down for text.
Photo Guzman

Output: Moves Beating, ...
Nine Inch Nails/Perry Farrell, 1994. Two articles run simultaneously over ten pages. Facing Perry Farrell is Trent Reznor.
Hot For Teacher, 1994. Type is leaning towards the teacher.
(the article is about rock stars' lustful memories of teachers). Photo Floris Andrea.

Get Your MOTOR Runnin. Head Out the Hiway

by Mark Woodlief

An independent bands typical tour vehicle is easily iden-
tifiable. Covered with bumper stickers, dust and finger-
streaked 'wash me' signs on the outside, the van is
almost always smelly and trash-strewn on the inside,
where a veritable jigsaw puzzle of loaded equipment lies
beneath a loft outfitted with a lumpy mattress. Some
bands do things differently. Olympias Beat Happening
used to criss-cross the US in a rental car, for example. While the rich and famous charter megabuses for
comfort, most groups settle for creative solutions to
beating the road blahs.

NEW
ORDER
CONTIN
UED

ALICE IN CHAINS
NICK CAVE
ELVIS COSTELLO
SPOONMAN
MULES DOGS
FASHION
TINDERSTICKS
SOUND IN PRINT
ADRIAN BELEW
REVIEWS
LAST PAGE

PHOTO: ALBERT WATSON

RAY GUN GOES ON ROAD

THE

music + style (the bible of)

ray

Goodbye Pixies, hello frank

dereche mode. the 1st interview

belly. ultra vivid scene. come. tommy stinson. the the. the sour dragons. john cale. redd kross meets debbie Gibson. etc.

march 1993 number 1 $3.50 u.s.a. $3.95 canada

^   < Contents page Issue 16, 1994. Photo Albert Watson
^   PJ Harvey, 1993. Illustration Geoff McFetridge. Photo Colin Bell
^ On the Road Again, 1994. Photos Kris Harnson [l], Doug Aitken [r]

ˇ
ˇ

Mixed Messages, 1993. Printouts of sections of type were used
ˇ   to explore   s p a c e s within characters, in
response to

title. Introduction is repeated twice, reflecting double

writing credits. Photo Anthony Artiago

619, 1993. Title refers to area code for San Diego, whose music scene is featured. Photo Steve Sherman >

Screaming Trees, 1993. Probably a little difficult to read, unless you are keen on the subject. The subtleness of this design involves a quiet laugh at optimum line-length.

Illustration Doug Aitken. Background photo Anne Brit Aase. Group photo David Hawkes.

Recording in **Soviet** Dis**union**, 1993. >
Body copy arrangement reflects the image.
Illustration Amy Guip.

ix
on
enie
n
e

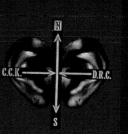

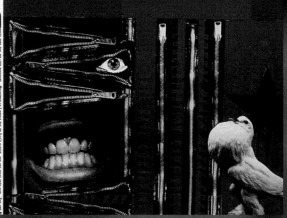

recording

in soviet

dis-union

by Lauren Agnelli

"Let CRAY-ZAY!" bellows Canadian video director Scott Dobson...

Raygun

Issue 25, 1995. The first time in magazine history that an inside story jumped to continue on the front cover.
Photo by Guy Aroch

R AYGUN.

*perry farrell
nine inch nails
joan jett
rev. horton heat*

*on th e road
the cramps*

agai n

Issue 17, 1994. Three images combined in Photoshop and Collage.
Photos Melanie McDaniel.
Plane: Dan Conway. Dog: Jason Lamotte

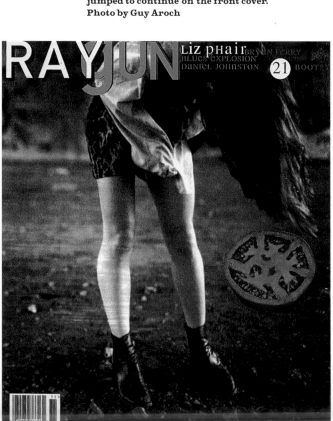

RAYJUN liz phair BRYAN FERRY
BLUES EXPLOSION
DANIEL JOHNSTON **21** BOOTS

Issue 21, 1994. Rejecting the nice color shots, a black and white Polaroid was used,
with visual pun on "hot tomato".
Photo Kevin Kerslake

R AYGU N,

ISSUE NUMBER 19 OF THE BIBLE OF MUSIC + STYLE AND THE END OF PRINT

JESUS
ANDMARYCHAIN
PRETEND
BACK TO SCHOOL
ERS
WITH
PAVEMENT, BAD
RELIGION, SU-
PERCHUNK, ETC.

Issue 19, 1994. Band picture is small, below the barcode, undermining the normal emphasis on cover photography. Ray Gun logo featured was drawn by Ed Fella, taken from a poster he designed announcing a talk by Carson.
Photo Colin Bell

y

Iggy. 1993. Photo Matt Mahurin

Sonic Youth on the road, 1993.
Photo Alan Messer. Line art Steve Tozzi
∨

on the road with
S o n i c   Y o u t h

New York City
17 March 1993
It's the middle
of March, and we
Sonic Youths have
been out on the
road almost
continuously since
last August, one
series of gigs
leading into the
next. It feels
like we've been
gone forever. Our
passports are
full of exotic
stamps from all
over the globe.
Recent travels
along our tour
tour have taken
us around the
U.S., across
Europe and to
the Pacific rim
Australia, New
Zealand,
Singapore, Japan,
Hawaii, and back
west from LA to
Seattle. A big
sonic hello to all
of you who came
to our shows,
and also to the
bands we toured
with, some of
whom were Royal
Trux, Pavement,
Jon Spencer Blue
Explosion, Huggy
Bear, Cell, Dead
C, Mudhoney,
Nick Cave, Iggy
Stooge, Boredoms
and Sebadoh.
What follows are
some stray
notes,
observations and
scribbles from
this sonic
touring.

guid

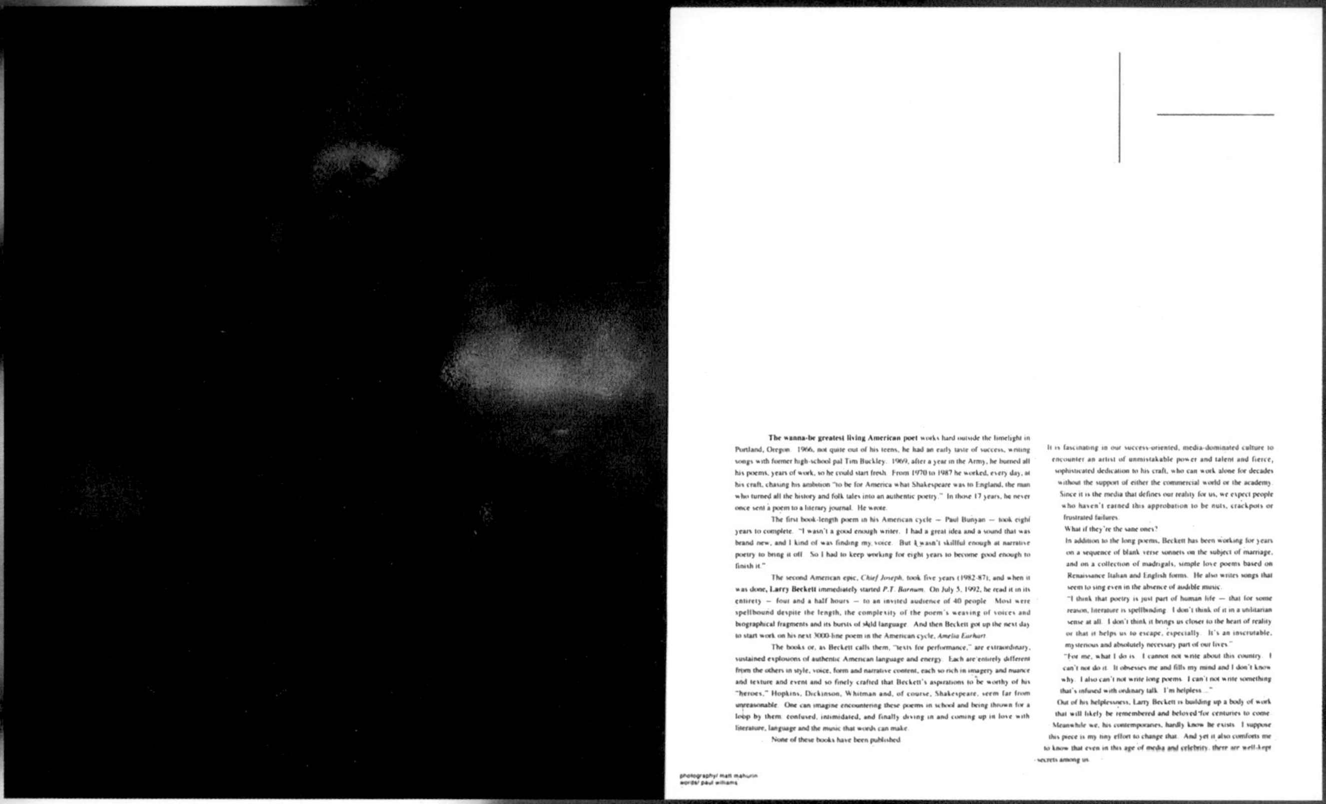

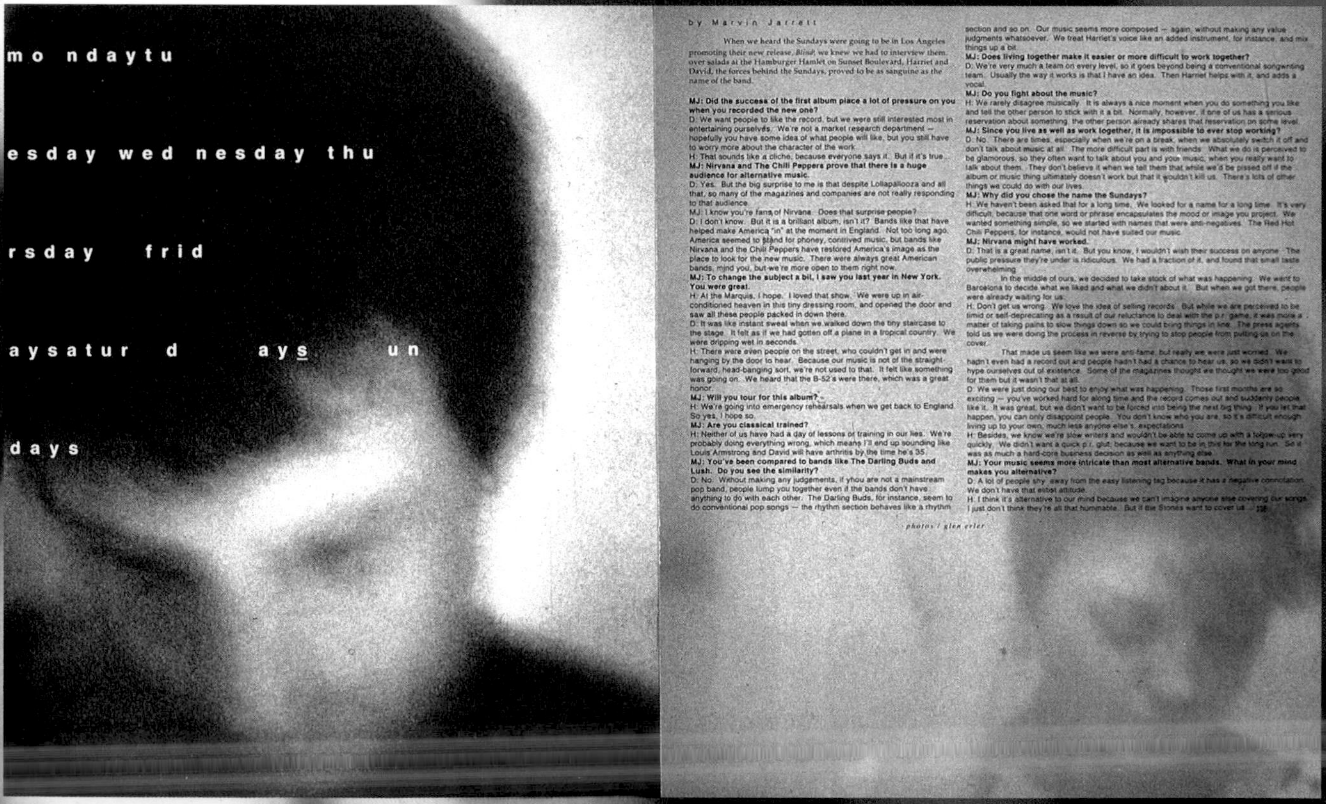

mo ndaytu

esday wed nesday thu

rsday frid

aysatur d ays un

days

by Marvin Jarrett

The Best Unknown Poet In America, 1993. Given the subject, the title was omitted. Photo Matt Mahurin

The Sundays, 1993. Opening page lists the days of the week, with a line below the S of

Sunday giving an understated hint of a title.

The Shamen, 1993. Two spreads from three. One page is completely blank on opener. Curved column idea begins here, a much copied element of Ray Gun.

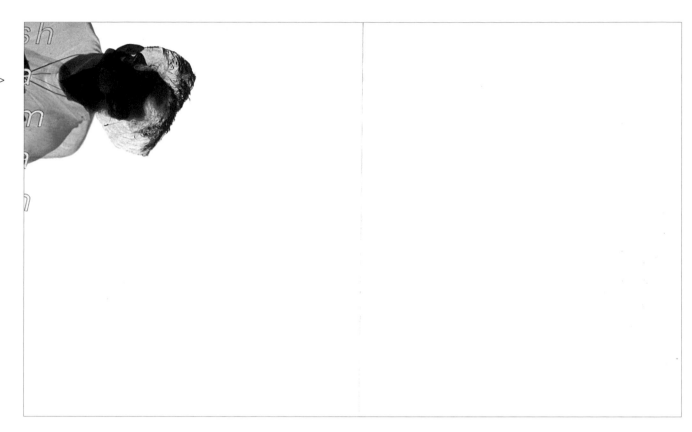

trying to do the same. If they don't they lose. In the case of the LA Shamen show they lost.

Avalon Attractions Les Boursais had originally booked this Shamen show for the Shrine Auditorium, capacity 6500. Last year he did the Spruce Goose extravaganza and was hoping to go in one bigger. But when ticket sales failed to break the 100 mark he understandably wanted out.

Promoter Philip Blaine of Kingfish now Moveable Feast Inc. picked up the show moved it to a smaller venue and was left with only seven days to promote it.

'I've been doing raves for a long time and the Shamen show wasn't really a rave.' he admits. 'If I knew I was going to do that gig a month ago it would have been in a warehouse. There would have been 5,000 people there, and tons of extra curricular stuff going on besides the band. But a full scale rave takes a lot of production and promotion. Usually when you confirm a show you put an ad in the LA Weekly, you put heavy promotion on KROQ, you give away a bunch of tickets. You do a lot.' Boursais did a little but he didn't really get behind it with a really good four color flyer or anything like that.

'It was okay.' says C of the gig the next day as he and Colin sit in their San Francisco hotel room awaiting soundcheck. **'America's just really behind. Everything here is just rock and roll now. It's really backward.'**

It's exactly this 'backward' mentality — the brainless, beer swilling whine men waving their fists, slam dancing, stage diving and all the other macho posturing that accompanies a rock concert — that Colin and C strive to transcend.

There is definitely a shamanic tradition in rock and roll. Colin says: 'Some performers were being real, especially in the 60's with Morrison and Hendrix and all that. But those kinds of performers were going poetry and virtuosity and information in the music, and that was shamanic. Most rock and roll is just an ego thing, with everyone just focusing on the person up there.'

'There's no drawing in the people so that it is a unified thing with rock because it's all me, me me.' C picks up. 'What we're creating here is a happening for everyone. There's not a head performer because that is a domination type thing. We're not like that. We're more an influence than the leader. We're just part of the whole experience.'

The band is the first to admit that not every American audience is open minded enough to receive the Shamen message. **Even in supposedly hip New York City,** the band found themselves halfway through the set before the audience caught on. 'After a while.' C smiles 'they can't help but be empowered by the rhythms.'

'But there are concerts where they're into it from the first beat.' says Colin. 'They're ready for it. They've come for it. They know they're going on a journey and they're ready.'

Increasingly, says Blaine, these cities are smaller, like

(Colin relates:)

There's a lot of pe here who underst They know what's g on. Just wait til you the show tonight.

DANCE

Bootsy Collins, 1994. Photo D. Altman Flescher

Jellyfish, 1993. Hippy band, off-centre, flower. Photo Moriane.

Background Meredith Parmelee

Choice Comes to Pensacola, 1994. Photo Eric Lynn [top l]. Illustration Nicky, [bottom l], Beregausky [r]

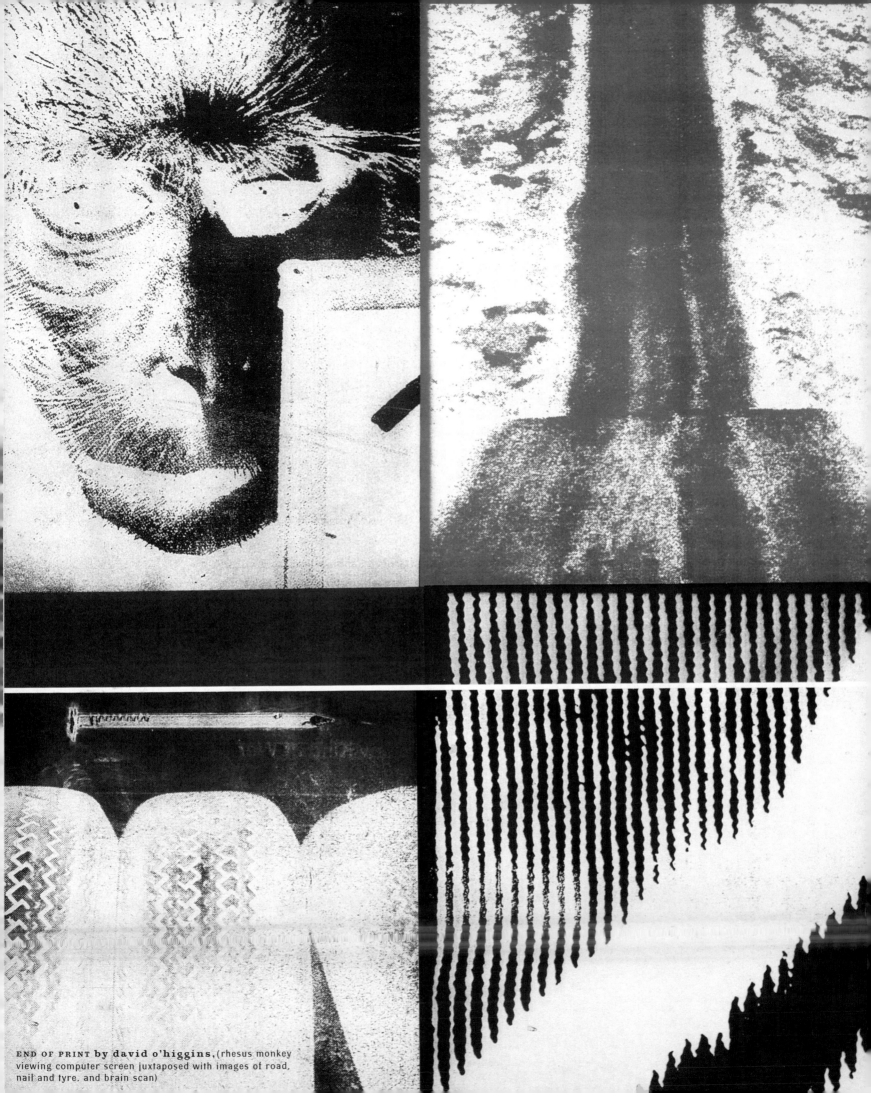

END OF PRINT **by david o'higgins,** (rhesus monkey viewing computer screen juxtaposed with images of road, nail and tyre, and brain scan)

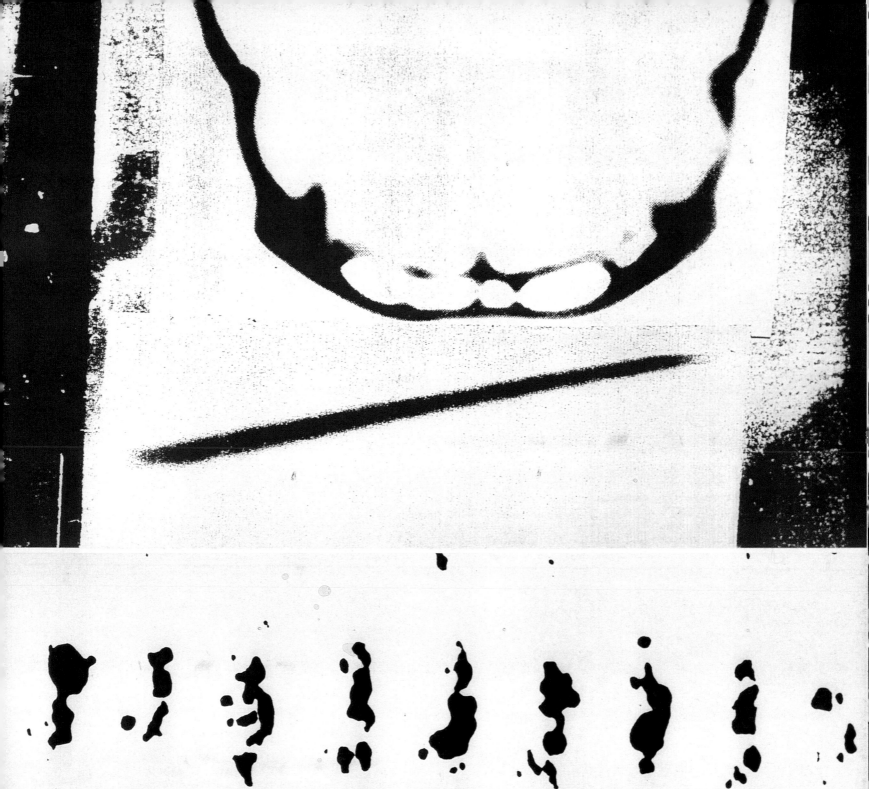

end of print **by david o'higgins** (image of human skull juxtaposed with abstracted computer screen and road marking)

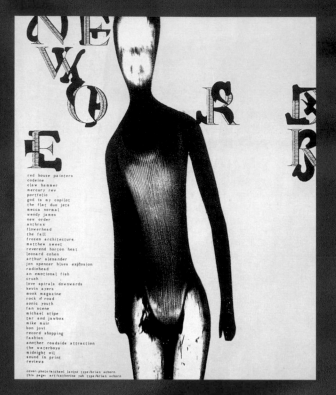

NEW ORDERS

red house painters
codeine
claw hammer
mercury rev
portfolio
god is my copilot
the flat duo jets
mecca normal
wendy james
new order
anthrax
flowerhead
the fall
frozen architecture
matthew sweet
reverend horton heat
leonard cohen
arthur alexander
jon spencer blues explosion
radiohead
an emotional fish
crush
love spirals downwards
kevin ayers
monk magazine
rock 'n' road
sonic youth
fan scene
michael stipe
tar and jawbox
mike muir
bon jovi
record shopping
fashion
another roadside attraction
the waterboys
midnight oil
sound in print
reviews

cover: photo/michael levine type/brian schorn
this page: art/catherine rub type/brian schorn

Mecca NORMAL

Band achieves international notoriety after 21 tours and four albums

By Denise Sheppard

After 21 years, four albums, a pair of EP's and innumerable singles, Mecca Normal (vocalist Jean Smith and guitarist David Lester) are finally receiving international notoriety. "When we released our first record in '86," recalls Lester, "people would sometimes compare Jean's singing to Yoko Ono, and that was meant as a derisive comment. Now the times have changed so much that this reference is intended to be a compliment. We've been putting out records for years, but they are fundamentally the same."

"We pretty much cleared rooms," says Smith, speaking of the band's early performances. "That was our main function. So if that happened we knew we were on the right track. It almost feels fickle now that people like us, because we're doing exactly the same thing. I have to ask myself, 'Well, what phenomenon is this?' We were not accepted and that was an inspiration, right?"

Conversely, it is that very same live show which appeals to—and requires—so many fans. Onstage, Lester is a man of few words and many actions. His extremely physical playing is simultaneously beautiful and uncomfortable to watch. Jean is also mesmerizing live. Swaying, chanting, even dropping the microphone in mid-verse in regular fare, preferring instead to sing while walking out amongst the crowd. "I view what Jean and I do as a musical form of civil disobedience," says Lester.

"You don't play the game, but instead you try to make what I consider a social change within the scope of a musical format."

After years of releasing hard-to-find singles and EP's, a 22-track collection, Jarred Up, has recently been issued. By no means, however, is it to be confused with a "Mecca Normal's Greatest Hits," as Jean is quick to explain "The songs are just literally the likes of 'Man Thinks Woman,' 'This Is Different' and 'Strong White Male,' much of it pulled from the band's early days.

An as-yet-untitled full-length disc of recent material is slated for September (Smith describes it as "very different—sort of energy and quite a bit darker"), followed by late of touring. Smith is also releasing her first book—entitled I Can Hear You—sometime this fall. When asked how long the pair can imagine their productivity lasting, Smith says the sky's no limit. "I'm sure we'll be working together when we're in our eighties. It's that kind of relationship. We understand each other and have a similar desire to inspire other people to do something or feel something."

They're arrived. David Lester and Jean Smith

We've been putting out records for years, but they are fundamentally the same... It almost feels fickle now that people like us because we are doing exactly the same thing.

26 • RAY GUN, JUNE/JULY, 1993   PHOTOGRAPH BY W.A. HOLCHER

e etc

Gun

gy

SONIC YOUTH
...and t...

by Andy Jenkins
Photos by Spike Jonze
Fax by Mark Newman

To Kill Your idols is an idea of heroic proportion. Other idols might make. Sonic Youth made before anyone cared to record anything other than themselves. One that had to be released by a European company (Zensor).

That was almost ten years ago. Sonic Youth have just released their album number two for DGC, *Dirty*, and are still firmly wedged into the role of alternative rock's top dogs despite the major-label bidding. Ten years have seen them idolized and imitated by countless numbers.

To Kill Your idols... But this is understandable considering Sonic Youth. Structurally they've had standing after so much time. Solid walls of manipulated noise, inhabited not so much by what are normally called songs, but rather by waves of sound that bend and twist into aural experiences. Stories with layers of texture that rub together to create a smoke that engulfs you like a damp cocoon. Shit. I'm sorry—that sounds pretty heavy. Well that's the weight I had to carry into the interview with Thurston Moore (guitar/vocals), Kim Gordon (bass/vocals), Steve Shelley (drums) and Lee Ranaldo (guitar/vocals). My, yeah...Sonic Youth. How I've made out an idolizer. Damn.

I felt I might succeed at meeting the creators of so many stories dissolved quickly. 635 Govier Street in Los Angeles is the main location for the *100%*, the first single/video from *Dirty*. In that spot is a small house that the band, about 20 extras and a modest film crew (including Spike Jonze) were inhabiting this day. How did I get here?

Sonic Youth, two hopeful minimalistic mirrors of a skateboarding and had somehow acquired a copy of a feature length video Spike had done on Plan B skateboards. Spike gets a message on his answering machine from Thurston, which he mistook for a prank call until Kim called back. They fixed the Blind

idols god on time

ronic youth

BUTTER

Sonic Youth

NY is needed, you see, and that is why New York will be renamed Ray Gun.

Claes Oldenburg, 1961

SUBSCRIBE
800.229.4GUN

< Contents page, 1993. Type design by Cranbrook student Brian Schorn mixes letters before and after the actual character chosen to generate new form.

Art Catherine Yuh.

< Mecca Normal, 1993. Normal by name, normal by layout: a duplicate of a page from Rolling Stone

Manic Street Preachers, 1993. Type boxes constructed for building the layout were included in the finished piece. Photo Colin Bell
<

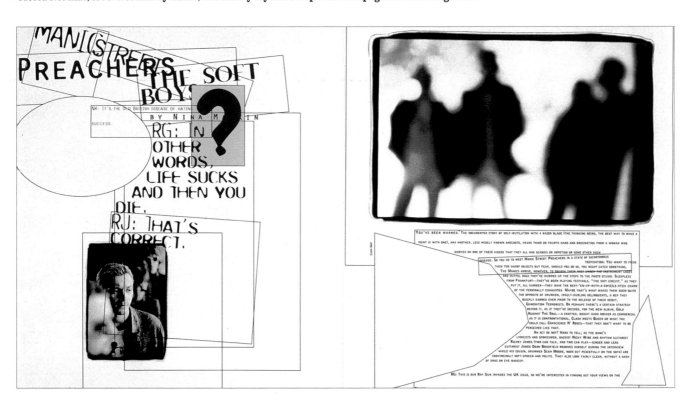

< Sonic Youth, 1992. Character of illustration reflected in title [written with left hand] over hard copy of article. Illustration James Fish

< Subscription ad, 1993.
Old magazine image collage DC

<
Richard Thompson, 1993. Includes found art that empathizes with the music. Photo Greg Allen. Background Geoff McFetridge

by Anita Sarko

backbeat(the sound of) THE BEATLES

∧

Too Much Joy, 1992. First paragraph of

article completely obliterated by

overlapping, repeated type.

second paragraph, It reads OK from

second paragraph,

second paragraph, though...

∧

Backbeat, 1994. Deliberately cropped

out John Lennon from old Beatle card.
Backbeat, 1994. Leading shifts

throughout article

scar
la
nta
hopping
ch xtra
arge
Ning Mallon

I n a

...searched around xtra
...go lead singer Darren
...Eagleson's head is not a fashion
...tipoison It's not intended as the top
...glorious headwear for BBD Really it's
...tzny tide bondage Who happened was
...gripi and his cap store in their neighbourhood
...particular to pick up some snacks when they
...ly accosted by an elderly lady who insisting that the
...belonged to her whacked Darren upside the head with
...bag of frozen bagels So he s not hoping to launch a trend he s
...ly recovering from an internal hemorrhage

        Being trendy in any way shape or form is in fact
... antithetic to all of xtra large   In addition to Darren that's Robert Melrose
...tison 19 who plays bass and is Bob is you Josh Freese who plays drums and
...xtrain Anthony Fitzgerald who plays guitar and produced the band's debut LP, the strange,
...singularly gutsy but grippy right but incorrigible Now I Eat Them

        We make a point of staying away from whatever's popular. Darren says. But that doesn't
...they don't know how to have a good time in the high style realm of Eagleson's in Westwood which has been serving
big and tall men since 1887

        I don't know what I was thinking xtra large are not Boo Yaa Tribe or even Luther Vandross after a binge. But I've always wanted a
...real reason to enter that most mysterious of male domains the big and tall men's clothing shop and xtra large provided the perfect excuse. I don't know what they were
...thinking either but they agreed to drive up from Orange County. We meet over mugs of iced latte at the theme-keeping Big   Tall bookstore and cafe in West Hollywood and
...of while waiting for Josh who'd spent the morning spitting grapes and sour cream for a friend's pixel camera in Venice.

        I begin to understand the extent of xtra large's adamant anti-fashionism. To strive for a certain image would be manicare. says Darren. We just do what
...do and if comes across the way it does. We re not trying to jump on some wacky alternative guys kind of thing.

        They are, however, nothing if not unconventional. Even in the way the band was formed. They all knew each other from around for years. and had at some
...one or another played together. but were each involved in a host of fairly viable projects. Big Drill Car, the Vandals Infectious Grooves

        It's been a totally backwards evolution. says Darren, who knows about science and stuff having graduated from UCI with a biology degree. Usually when
...you start a band you play live for like a year and then go record something.

        But we started as a recording entity first. We decided to do this because it gave us the chance to stretch out a little musically from the bands we were in
...do something completely a little off the wall that we couldn't do in, say, a punk rock or a pop context.

        In a further break from rock tradition, getting signed was not a priority. We were just doing what we liked to do and didn't put a lot of emotional weight

be an
...retor
We have a
...characteristics
...that aren't like
...Musicians Like us
...don't have ventured
...disease   Like being
...friends Warren leans over
...graphic rent and pornography
...Like being on nitro do it on cue
...Josh grinnes and we can go

        A chuckle hits Fitzgerald. In three of this things
...way women getting tinted this another looks on
...Paul Rangel. the good-humored assistant manager of
...Eagleson's Westwood branch watches us warmly silly
...large scurry about trying on outfits. Try for but and this nonstop
...manor hurriedly finish their business pill tone

        Look Oscar de la Terror cloth says slipping on a polka-dot
...short that reaches below his knees. Bob puts on a pair of classic Eddington trousers
...in which he could smuggle an entire family across the border

        My attitude about clothes is not to try to be cool and keep up with what's popular. Warren says
...dashing in a plaid top and patterned bonains Pump him full of helium, hang a basket from his crossbars and
...he could take us all for a champagne picnic in the sky. I'd rather just be retarded. Because whatever's lame is dying in the
...lame forever. it's the kind of thing you can stick with.

        The fashion-music connection is not lost to these gents. It just frightens them. The alternative is now the mainstream. All of a sudden you lose a bit of
...your identity. Bob observes, rounding out his monochromatic ensemble with a natty ascot. This whole mainstream alternative explosion thing is unsettling. It's good
...because we have an opportunity to be heard. but the alternative scene was the only place where you could express yourself and be artistic, and now it's become the new
...glam rock.

        It's terrifying. Darren agrees. adjusting his scarf bandito style to maximize the invisible man effect. You have alternative
...music, this whole scene that's been around forever and once it hits MTV and the charts and everything and the general public has access to it and
...it's into it, it's weird. When something becomes popular, the impact it has is bizarre. I just hope we don't get lumped in with the whole new wave of
...bands who were like Poison two years ago an now all cut their hair and wear shorts and combat boots.

        And how will you be paying for this? Paul inquires. Then he laughs. He's used to dealing with celebrity clientele. Among his
...regular customers is Mohammed. The Tallest Man In The World. who's eight-foot-one. Paul has to stand on a ladder to fit him.

        The last time Mohammed came by. Paul traced his hand on a gift box. He shows it to us. We're all impressed. Paul doesn't ask to

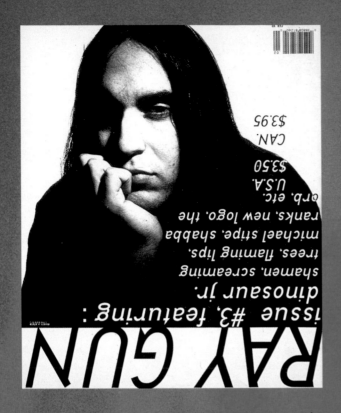

Issue three, 1993. This cover is upside down [the picture of J Mascis was upside down, a reflection of his emphatic disrespect for magazines]. Beginning of a period of changing logos

Fan scene, 1993. Lips from Hatch Show Print letterpress poster

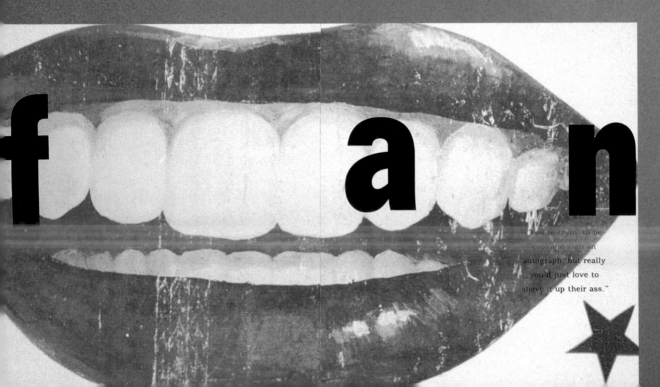

^
*On the road travel piece, 1993. Photo through windshield of Baja, Mexico, DC. On the road food, 1994. Juxtaposition of airline coding bag
sticker with food store image. Photo Aaron Tucker*

v

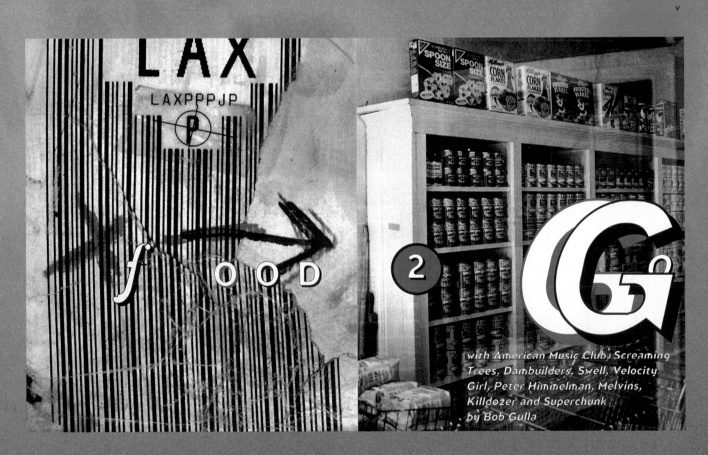

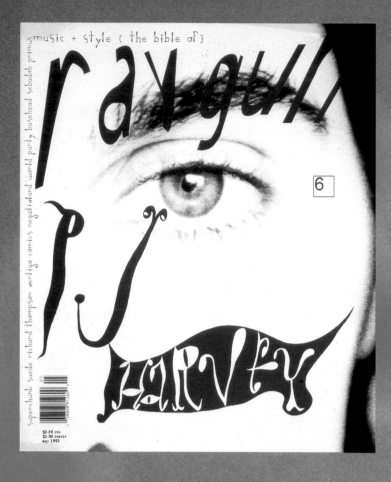

< Issue six, 1993.
Hand-lettering Calef Brown.
PJ Harvey photo Colin Bell

Tin Man, 1993.
Letterpress with broken characters used for headline.
Photo Scott Lowden
∨

Brian Eno, 1994. >
Interpretation of Eno's ambient sound with spare layout.
Photo Ophelia Chong

Is Techno Dead? 1994.
Title absorbed into the layout,
body copy generates major shapes across the spread,
empathizing the heavy techno mix.
Photo John Ritter >

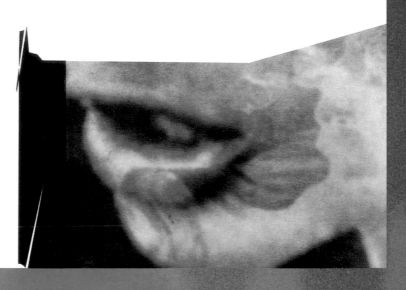

en

o

"Techno" used to be a prefix: technology, technocrat, technophobia. Coming from ancient Greek, 'techno' suggests both art and skill. What it suggests these days, however, is a dance sound that is produced almost exclusively with computer technology—sequencers, drum machines and digital synthesizers hooked together with MIDI cables and controlled by Macintosh, Atari or other PCs. Some call it "popurist" for its accessibility, others call it "cold" for its reliance on samples and synths. Whatever you call it, the sound has wormed its way into mainstream dance culture.

Listening to the techno compilations that are currently swamping the market, a problem soon becomes apparent. Since most are trying to fit into what is perceived to be a narrow sound, the selections are pretty narrow themselves. As some, this adds up to, "Techno music is dying fast," Rob DeStefano, director for house music label Tribal says, "Too many artists missed the one sound," and shifted.

DeStefano isn't alone in declaring techno D.O.A. in America—in fact, some of the very DJ/producers represented on the new compilations admit that they think techno is passé and are moving into different directions. But now that raves have emigrated from the UK and are starting to have an impact in the States, techno albums are coming out from record companies all over the map—not just the small labels (Instinct, Continuum, Nova/Mute), but majors (Rhino, Warner, Arista, CBS) are pumping out the sound.

Despite all its critics, the techno sound is still growing, whether through the efforts of the producers like the ubiquitous Moby or the new crop of dance music groups: 808 State, Digital Orgasm/Lords Of Acid, SunScreem. And the sound is clearly making friends in high places—the hit "Something Good" by Utah Saints was the first song ever to have a sample cleared for use by Kate Bush, while Madonna is rumored to be working on techno-styled cuts for her next album. This heavy-hitter attention has connected some major labels to push techno/rave as the new dance culture.

"Rave is the only dance culture for white people," says Lance Walden at Arista's Dance Department. "A lot of white kids are into hiphop, but it isn't their culture." This view is seconded by Rick Rubin's Def American imprint, which has opened an all-techno rave label, White Label Records. Since techno's biggest impact has been in Europe, with a mostly white audience, the labels assume that white American kids will take to in-an operating philosophy that alienates some people in the dance music community. "I don't think anyone goes out of their way to associate with just one kind of people, it's open to everybody," Tom Hayden, the producer of Zoo Rave, remarked. "I think open people listen to any form of music." New York DJ Heikki Plankton, editor of the clubzine Project X admits, "The first impact of techno was this hardcore, white jumping-up-and-down energy," but says "it's silly" to assume only whites will be interested.

LOOKING BACK...

Even older than with disco, a feature of techno culture is that there are no "stars." The DJ is the conduit, but "groups" are usually non-existent—names are slapped on a record at random by the producer. Ensembles like 808 State and Digital Orgasm are mad and put on a show, but they're not hero-worshiped event. It's still common for faceless producers to spend more glamorous "actors" to star in their videos instead, as happened with groups like the 1799 and the house group Black Box. Chicago producer/remixer/DJ Mark Imperial. "Does the end justify the means? I say yes," he says. "if in the end the product that you're able to present the public is an enjoyable one, if it fails, don't do it."

Raves were slow to take root in America, and many in the US record industry either took a "wait and see" approach or assumed that techno was a "fad," as DeStefano puts it. But a small rave underground started to emerge...

techno was regarded as fringe in the mid US late Eighties, when it split off from the house sound on small dance music labels in Detroit (especially +8 Records) and Chicago. Though it started in the US, the deep, thudding kick drum and square, streamlined sound made the greatest impact in Europe. Darren Partington of England's 808 State says, "In the mid Eighties we were into hiphop, but it was really the Chicago and Detroit stuff that inspired us—Fingers and Derek May. We [had been] waiting for something to come along."

Meanwhile, Belgian producer Praga Khan of Lords of Acid says, "The first time I heard of techno was when I saw the techno compilation on Ten Records in England. Responding to techno in a way they never did to hiphop, the 'Belgians started to forge their own variety, which many call the beginning of 'true' techno. Rather than playing up the Kraftwerk influence of the Detroit techno-house, Praga says, the Belgian techno brought out something new. "The Electronic Body Music, like Front 242, Nitzer Ebb, stuff like that."

Europeans took their techno far more seriously than the American originators did, with enclaves and labels in Belgium (Antler, Subway), Germany (R & S Records, Hart House) and England. It's generally agreed that the Euro-techno became harder and edgier, while the American variety is more soulful. "We have the black influence and they don't," says Minneapolis DJ Brett Edgar, mastermind of the group Red Red Groovy. "The techno thing in America came out of house, which is a black thing, and it became big in Europe. These guys went off on it. They pulled the ideas but added a European perspective, which tends to be more new-wavish or progressive."

BURIED IN THE RAVE...

What happened next was a weird mix of dance and rock culture. England raves, word-of-mouth dance parties where the ecstasy flowed like wine. A rock phenomenon revolving around the Manchester scene, remixes of songs by the likes of Happy Mondays were twerked with break beats (i.e. hiphop beats speeded up). But raves soon morphed into an electronic dance culture powered with cuts by producers like the Orb, the Shamen and Bizarre Inc., and DJs were the crucial link to the public. "The knowledge of the average club-goer is really strong," says Darren of 808 State. "If you're involved [in the music] you have to know it all." The raves were dance happenings akin to the massive parties organized by sound systems like the Soul To Soul crew, but without the soul.

techno was regarded as fringe in the mid US late Eighties emerge, with kids hiring a DJ for the night and organizing their own parties. Problems with licensing and underage drinking often halted parties before they could start, but raves are now occurring with more and more frequency. By the end of last year, raves were starting to become big business—a New Years rave party at Knott's Berry Farm in California is said to have brought 17,000 people.

In an effort to explain the appeal of raves, comparisons to rock archetypes are everywhere. "I kind of equate the raves to the Sixties, with the flowers and things like that," says Hassen. "It's a gift that type of young enthusiastic people going out to them and having a great time." Others, like Edgar, see a closer affiliation to the punk explosion. The DIY aspect that drove many non-singers and non-players into pure goods is echoed now in non-musicians turning to the accessible and relatively cheap technology that is being harnessed to make the percolating rhythms of techno. "Half these kids make this shit because they got their dad's computer," he says. "This is the next step of the technology—anybody, where anyone can do it."

LOOKING FORWARD...

And this is when DJs and producers start to sound wistful, pie-in-the-sky. With the music starting to progress away from the generic sounds, DJ Keoki heralds the coming of techno-inspired wonders. "You wouldn't have a Doctectu Twins if it weren't for punk," he says, "but they're not punk rock. You wouldn't have the Human League, the Cure, Peter Murphy, the Sugarcubes. These are all extended veins of the punk rock explosion, and I think techno is the same thing. Boom! Something happens and it changes dance music, and it trails off in different directions, but it's never the same."

He's right. Dance cuts are coming out with a techno flavor but with elements borrowed from house and even rock music, forming all sorts of off-shoots: "Tribal" adds African percussion to techno beats; "Trance" is more keyboard based, like Tangerine Dream with a beat. Beyond the music itself, these producers are excited by the possibilities, because as the very name suggests, techno music is married to technology, and plugs in easily with a variety of media formats. Some look forward to more explicit multi-media knows or a full-scale marriage of techno to cyberspace and virtual reality.

As soon as the techno sound was snapped up, its days were numbered—it was only a matter of time before techno began to be absorbed into the mainstream dance music. "When you hear Gloria Estefan remixes with a techno feel," laughs Edgar, "you know it's been swallowed up by the big monster of pop music." By now it's even hard to get anyone to agree what "techno" means. "I have a difficult time using the word techno, because everybody has such a different idea," complains Picchiotti. "There's rave, trance. To me techno is [now] the umbrella definition for that genre of music."

So the simple answer to the "Is techno dead?" question that rumbles around has little to do with sales and groups. "It makes 'em seem stupid to say techno's dead because techno obviously is dead," says Keoki. The mistake comes from viewing music from a marketing standpoint where it describes a static entity. It's made its mark, and even as it continues to evolve and influence other styles, the sound moves on, even as the raves continue. "A lot of DJs across the country are planning rave parties this summer," Hayden says. "You might want to catch the rave before it morphs into something else."

techno dead ?

next spread] On left, 'pagination' in video. The process of eliminating >
in the edit bay while directing a commercial.
On right, issue eight contents page, 1993. Uses pagination sheet from issue three,
overlaid with new contents.

TURN

OVER

OVER

you can

1-800-66-RYDER

lust.
tim

TURN

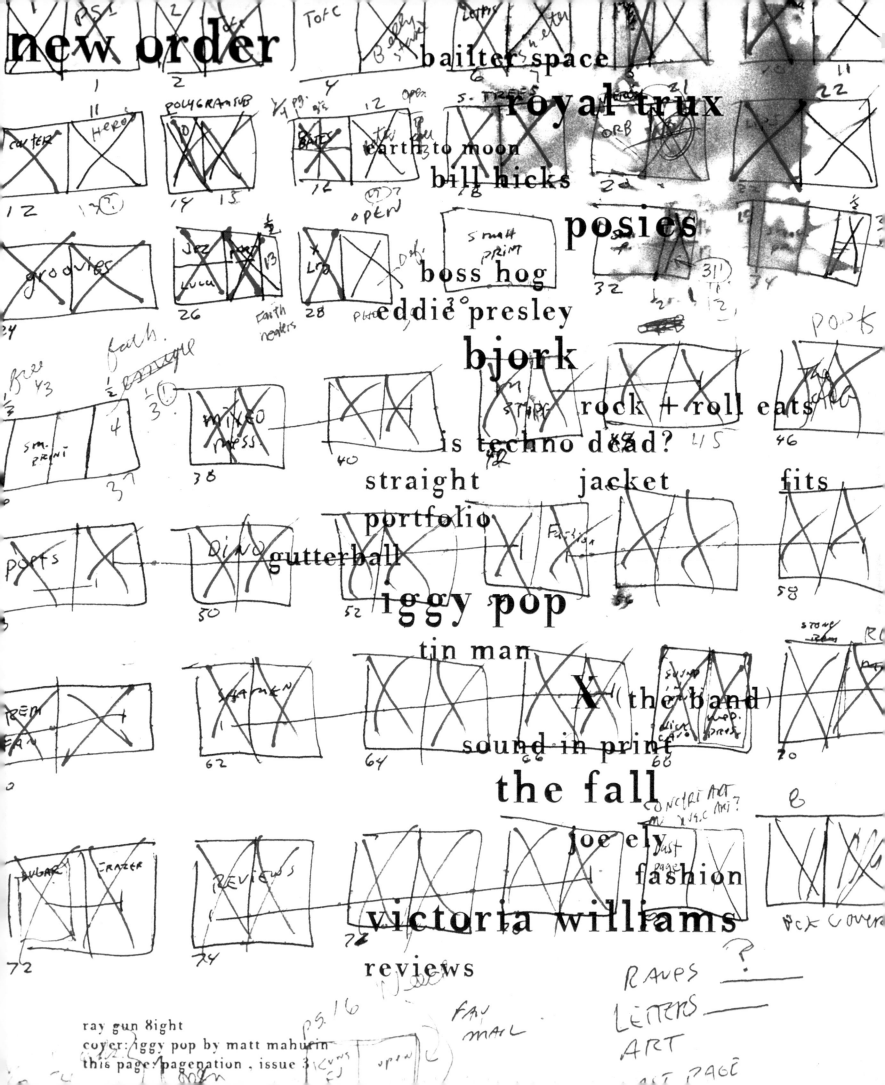

new order

bailter space

royal trux

earth to moon

bill hicks

posies

boss hog

eddie presley

bjork

rock + roll eats

is techno dead?

straight   jacket   fits

portfolio

gutterball

iggy pop

tin man

X (the band)

sound in print

the fall

joe ely

fashion

victoria williams

reviews

ray gun 8ight
cover: iggy pop by matt mahurin
this page: pagenation , issue 3

fRAnkblack

by Nina M...

Why be Frank Black, Black Francis, Slash, the Edge, Ice Whatever, etc.? "Because you can," Frank Black says. "It's part of rock 'n' roll, like wearing the leather jacket.

It's just schtick."

Why Frank Black specifically is simple. "It's a totally new stage name that makes more sense than the other one did. People never really got my original stage name right." He smiles. "They don't know if I'm Black, they don't know if I'm Francis. ...So I said, 'Oh, forget it, I've gotten what I could out of that.

It's time for a new name."

< Frank Black, 1993.

Sequence

of

spreads

featuring

reversal

of

image

out

of

text.

Hand-lettering Edd Patton.

Photo Mike Halsband

photo: Peter Morello   stylist: Jill Spector

^

Bryan Ferry, 1994. All type Zapf Dingbat.
Photo Peter Morello

>

Compulsion, 1994.
Headline, text and image
echo spatial relationships.
Photo Michael Wong

**Survival Research
Laboratories,** 1993.
DC font based on scanning
fingers.
When article was printed
out, only upper case
appeared.
The effect seemed
sympathetic to content so it
ran, with article
repeated legibly on the
following page

Ray Gun mail >

Ween, 1994.
Bizarre band.
Weakest element is the
band photo, so downplayed.
Photos Melanie Acevedo

**Photograph/Illustration
by Paul Weston**

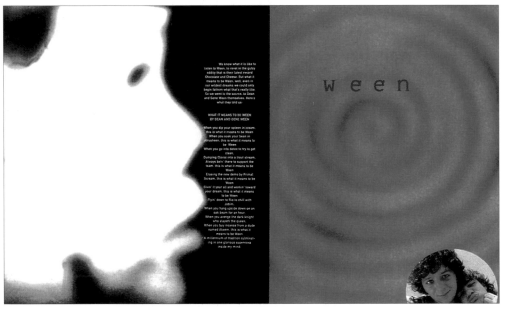

London fashion, 1995. Photos Corinne Day >

[Waterboys], 1993.
Magazine had to be pulled
apart to reveal title

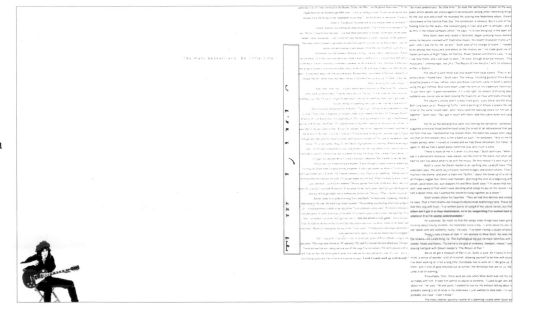

BY MARK WOODLIEF

They're young, talented, noisy, and alive, which is more than one can say for most monolithic rock groups that dot the American landscape in 1993. They're so scrappy and friendly, on a first-name basis—Jim, Mac, Laura and Jon—with any one who's bought any of their records in the last four years. Collectively, they're one entity, Superchunk. Chapel Hill, NC's answer to the DIY ethic that's still surviving and being reshaped whenever an instrument winds up in the hands of anybody who just wants to wrestle the weapon to the ground.

Superchunk wields its weaponry—two guitars, bass, drums and voice—with purpose. Abrasive, loud, tense, Superchunk brashly goes where plenty of bands, from Hüsker Dü to Mac's mid-late Eighties project Slush Puppies, have gone before. Then Superchunk goes further. The question, as Superchunk proposes on its latest release, *On The Mouth*, is how fast? But don't get bogged down in the asking, the question is really a riddle.

"We have so much to answer for/So sick of talking about it," "For Tension."

Nobody in the band seems to mind doing interviews, but an interviewer does get the sense that Superchunk's members would rather be hanging out by a basketball court or relaxing on a warm day in a Chapel Hill park. Laura hates questions from naive writers who want to know what it was like to produce Superchunk's second LP, *No Pocky For Kitty*. While she's credited with producing "with eyes closed" and sitting "in the right chair," the plain truth is that noise figurehead Steve Albini captured the band's sound at his basement studio in Chicago.

"Seems like people today need a damn shot of reality. Maybe it shouldn't take shock tactics, expletives, etc. to get people's attention, but apparently it helps WAKE UP or FUCK OFF."—Mac's liner notes in the *Evil I Do Not* singles box set, 1987.

"2000 volts of common sense"—etched in Slushpuppies' "Assimilated"/"Lost At Ten" single.

It's 1987 and what we today call **"the Chapel Hill scene"** isn't. Plenty of national acts ran through the Triangle (Raleigh, Durham and Chapel Hill form an obtuse geographic triangle). MTV sent a camera crew to the Hill the previous year to capture the zany antics of Flat Duo

PARLIAMENT
AND THE
BEAT a history of
uk tec

"MAN HAS BEEN DANCING SINCE THE DAWN OF TIME. IN MANY PRIMITIVE SOCIETIES, THE DANCING WOULD START OFF AS PART OF A RITUAL BUT GRADUALLY TAKE ON AN IMPETUS OF ITS OWN AND, GROWING WILDER AND WILDER, SOMETIMES LAST SEVERAL DAYS."

TODAY'S TEENAGERS ARE ONLY INTERESTED IN ONE THING: THE BEAT.

"I FIRMLY BELIEVE THAT PEOPLE CAN, AND DO, HAVE REVELATORY EXPERIENCES ON THE DANCE FLOOR."
COLIN ANGUS, THE SHAMEN

BY ANDREW SMITH

Superchunk, 1993.< opposite top
Superchunk, 1993. In reversing the title out
of the body copy, chunks of text disappear
and chunks are created. The article is still
readable, if fractured.
Photo Michael Halsband

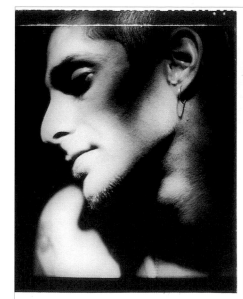

Perry Farrell, 1993.>
Great photo
by Merlyn Rosenberg – so it was
used twice. Overlaid with Hatch
Show Print devil [a subject
brought up in the article]

UK techno music, 1993.< opposite bottom left
UK techno music, 1993.Deliberately harsh
feel responds to music.
Photos [l to r] Rex Features, Liz Tobias

< opposite bottom right
Launch Issue, 1992. Carson cut his finger
during hurried paste-up, hence blood-
spattering

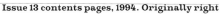

Issue 13 contents pages, 1994. Originally right   turning to left. Illustration Heidi Nelms

< Teenage fan club, 1993.
Photos Colin Bell

Songs In the Key Of Life, 1994.
Photo Alan Messer >

< Morrissey, 1994.
Mystery of artist is hinted at. Form partly driven out of type.
Form partly driven out of type.
This issue (14) was the first not pasted up,
but was sent in digital form to the color separator.
This encouraged greater freedom in exploring color.
Photo Chris Cuffaro.

Cocteau Twins, 1993.
Photo Mary Scanlon >

issue **2** emf by david Sims
issue **4** frank Black by michael Halsband
issue **8** iggy Pop by matt Mahurin
issue **16** layne Staley by cynthia Levine
issue **18** lush by michael Lavine
issue **22** keith Richards by alan Messer

< The Fall, 1993.
Photo Colin Bell

Kate Bush, 1993.
Art Ed Garcia >

Songs in the Key of Life

It might have been a chord, a voice, a chorus. Maybe just a look, an attitude, a concept...

Let's say you're a teen, pulling into a compromising position in the backseat of Dad's wagon — a song comes on the radio, you've heard a thousand times before, yet somehow, amid the passionate musing and slobbering and groping and uncertainty, it sounds so astounding, so enlightening, you swear you've never heard it quite that way before.

Unless you're a lifestyle living in a peat bog somewhere, music of some sort has guided your life with a tender... track... a accompaniment... marking the different phases you've been through. Most likely, at some point along your journey, music assumed such an essential role it actually overwhelmed you... taking over your thoughts, influencing your decisions, helping you see, giving you direction when you thought none existed.

We wanted to find out what songs some of today's rock 'n' rollers would single out as revelatory, the sounds they heard that changed their lives wholly and irrevocably. Here's what a few of them said.

BY BOB GULLA

PHOTO: ALLEN MESSER / WATCH SHOW PRINT

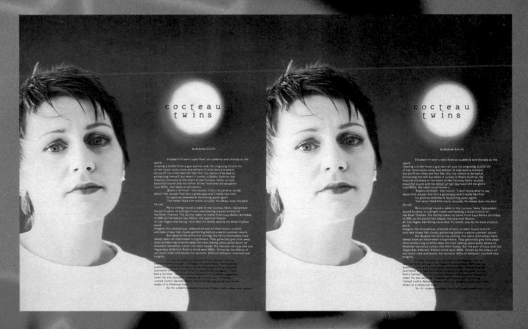

cocteau twins

by Andrew Smith

Elizabeth Fraser's eyes flash as suddenly and sharply as the spark...

We're sitting round a table in the Cocteau Twins' September Sound Studios, in a bright room overlooking a quiet stretch of the River Thames...

KATE B

UTMOST O SERVIC

Of course, if such treatment you can't endure,
You'd better stay home where you'll be secure.

B SYSTEM

WORDS UP

BANDS OF P

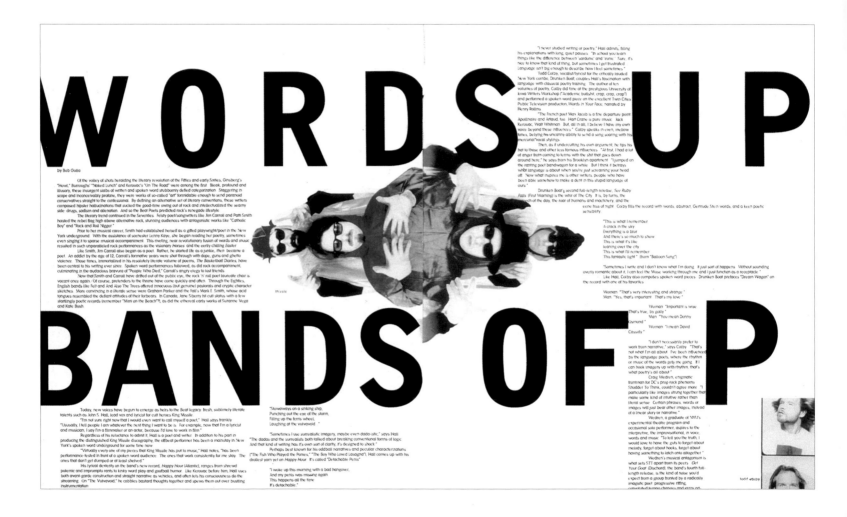

by Bob Guiza

Of the volley of shots heralding the literary revolution of the Fifties and early Sixties, Ginsberg's "Howl," Burroughs' "Naked Lunch" and Kerouac's "On The Road" were among the first. Bleak, profound and illusory, these insurgent slabs of written and spoken word stubbornly defied categorization. Staggering in scope and inconceivably profane, they were works of so-called "art" formidable enough to send paranoid conservatives straight to the confessional. By defining an alternative set of literary conventions, these writers composed hipster hallucinations that sucked the good-time swing out of rock and intellectualized the seamy side: drugs, sadism and alienation. And so the Beat Poets predicted rock's renegade lifestyle.

The literary trend continued in the Seventies. Feisty poet/songwriters like Jim Carroll and Patti Smith hoisted the rebel flag high above alternative rock, stunning audiences with antagonistic works like "Catholic Boy" and "Rock and Roll Nigger."

Prior to her musical career, Smith had established herself as a gifted playwright/poet in the New York underground. With the assistance of sometimes Lenny Kaye, she began reading her poetry, sometimes even singing it to sparse musical accompaniment. This riveting, near revolutionary fusion of words and music resulted in such unparalleled rock performances as the visionary Horses and the eerily chilling Easter.

Like Smith, Jim Carroll also began as a poet. Rather, he started life as a junkie, then became a poet. Those times, immortalized in his resolutely literate volume of poems, The Basketball Diaries, have been central to his writing ever since. Spoken word performances followed, as did rock accompaniment, culminating in the audacious bravura of "People Who Died," Carroll's angry elegy to lost friends.

Now that Smith and Carroll have drifted out of the public eye, the rock 'n' roll poet laureate chair is vacant once again. Of course, pretenders to the throne have come quickly and often. Through the Eighties, English bands like Felt and And Also The Trees offered innocuous (but genuine) pastorals and cryptic character sketches. More convincing in a literate sense were Graham Parker and the Fall's Mark E. Smith, whose acid tongues resembled the defiant attitudes of their forbears. In Canada, Jane Siberry hit cult status with a few startlingly poetic records (remember "Mimi on the Beach"?), as did the ethereal early works of Suzanne Vega and Kate Bush.

Today, new voices have begun to emerge as heirs to the Beat legacy: fresh, sublimely literate talents such as John S. Hall, lead vox and lyricist for cult heroes King Missile.

"I'm not sure right now that I would even want to call myself a poet," Hall says frankly. "Usually, I tell people I am whatever the next thing I want to be is. For example, now that I'm a lyricist and musician, I say I'm a filmmaker or an actor, because I'd love to work in film."

Regardless of his reluctance to admit it, Hall is a poet and writer. In addition to his part in producing the distinguished King Missile discography, the offbeat performer has been a mainstay in New York's spoken word underground for some time now.

"Virtually every one of my pieces that King Missile has put to music," Hall notes, "has been performance-tested in front of a spoken word audience. The ones that work consistently for me stay. The ones that don't get dumped or at least shelved."

His lyrical dexterity on the band's new record, Happy Hour (Atlantic), ranges from shrewd polemic and impromptu rants to kinky word play and goofball humor. Like Kerouac before him, Hall uses both avant-garde construction and straight narrative as vehicles, and often lets his consciousness do the streaming. On "The Vulvavoid," he cobbles bastard thoughts together and spews them out over bustling instrumentation.

"Stowaways on a sinking ship,
Punching out the eye of the storm,
Filling up the ferris wheel,
Laughing at the vulvavoid."

"Sometimes I use surrealistic imagery, maybe even dada-istic," says Hall. "The dadas and the surrealists both talked about breaking conventional forms of logic. And that kind of writing has it's own sort of clarity, it's designed to shock."

Perhaps best known for his oddball narratives and peculiar characterizations ("The Fish Who Played the Ponies," "The Boy Who Loved Lasagna"), Hall comes up with his drollest yarn yet on Happy Hour. It's called "Detachable Penis."

"I woke up this morning with a bad hangover,
And my penis was missing again.
This happens all the time.
It's detachable."

"I never studied writing or poetry," Hall admits, filling his explanations with long, quiet pauses. "In school you learn things like the difference between 'aardunic' and 'zrunic.' Sure, it's nice to know that kind of thing, but sometimes I get frustrated. Language isn't big enough to describe how I feel sometimes."

Todd Colby, vocalist/lyricist for the critically lauded New York combo, Drunken Boat, couples Hall's fascination with language with classical poetry training. The author of ten volumes of poetry, Colby did time at the prestigious University of Iowa Writers Workshop ("Academic bullshit, crap, crap, crap") and performed a spoken word piece on the excellent Twin Cities Public Television production, Words in Your Face, narrated by Henry Rollins.

"The French poet Max Jacob is a fine departure point. Apollinaire and Artaud, too. Hart Crane is pure music. Jack Kerouac, Walt Whitman. But, all in all, I believe I have my own voice beyond these influences." Colby speaks in even, mellow tones, belying his uncanny ability to send a song soaring with his mercurial vocal stylings.

Then, as if undercutting his own argument, he tips his hat to these and other less famous influences. "At first, I had a lot of anger from coming to terms with the shit that goes down around here," he says from his Brooklyn apartment. "I jumped on the ranting poet bandwagon for a while. But I think it betrays what language is about when you're just screaming your head off. Now what inspires me is other writers, people who have been able somehow to make a dent in this stupid language of ours."

Drunken Boat's second full-length release, Sex Rudy Falls (First Warning) is the whit of The City. It is, by turns, the screech of the day, the roar of humans and machinery, and the eerie hiss of night. Colby fills the record with words, abstract, Gertrude Stein words, and a keen poetic sensibility.

"This is what I remember
A crack in the sky
Everything is a blur
And there's so much to show
This is what it's like
leaning over the city
This is what I'll remember
This fantastic light." (from "Balloon Sung")

"Sometimes I write and I don't know what I'm doing. It just sort of happens. Without sounding overly romantic about it, I can feel the Muse working through me and I just function as a receptacle."

Like Hall, Colby also composes spoken word pieces. Drunken Boat's "Dream Wagon" on the record with one of his favorites.

Woman: "That's very interesting and strange."
Man: "Yes, that's important. That's my love."

Woman: "Important is wise.
That's true, by golly."
Man: "You mean Donny Osmond."
Woman: "I mean David Cassidy."

"I don't necessarily prefer to work from narrative," says Colby. "That's not what I'm all about. I've been influenced by the language poets, where the rhythm or music of the words gets me going. If I can hook imagery up with rhythm, that's what poetry's all about."

Craig Wedren, enigmatic frontman for DC's prog-rock phenoms Shudder To Think, couldn't agree more. "I particularly like images strung together that make some kind of intuitive rather than literal sense. Certain phrases, words or images will just bear other images, instead of a linear story or narrative."

Wedren, a graduate of NYU's experimental theatre program and occasional solo performer, aspires to the interpretive, the improvisational, in voice, words and music. "To tell you the truth, I would love to have the guts to forget about melody, forget about hooks, forget about having something to latch onto altogether."

Wedren's musical antagonism is what sets STT apart from its peers. Get Your Goat (Dischord), the band's fourth full-length release, is the kind of noise you'd expect from a group fronted by a radically imagistic poet: progressive riffing, convoluted tempo changes and jazzy off-...

missile

todd wesby

Words Up: Band Of Poets/Great Expectations 1993. These two spreads show an experiment with the idea of pages work...

by Neil FeinEman

eX GREAT pectation s

OETS

A tALe of tWO

ro ck

st AR

st ARs

m, where one article runs onto the next [Great Expectations], emphasizes the linearity possible in sequential pages

the Xenice

photos dc

DAVID

16/21 graphic gennaio
FORTUNY
p al az zo
fortuny
19 CARSON

95

conversation

lewis blackwell

graphic
FORTUNY
PALAZZO
DAVID D
C   A Rtsionny
16/21 GENNAIO
19
9
5

22   January   1995 Pensione
Accademia Venice,   Italy

Lewis Blackwell You're redesigning the magazine, Ray Gun: tell me about it...

David Carson The problem is I haven't worked it through right now. It's turning out to be a bit of a challenge because there's no...you know, I always have trouble speaking person-to-person once that machine is on, I lose some of the...

L Well, there's nothing to redesign: is that it? It redesigns itself every month?

D Something like that. In a sense I feel it does, but in another sense it doesn't: there is a certain predictability to its unpredictability, I realize that. I feel it's time to change because there are too many magazines trying similar things. It will go simpler in some way...the obvious thing would be to give it a format and everything, go in completely the opposite direction. Like Neville [Brody] did with Arena, after The Face. But that would be too simple, boring, and completely counter to the design philosophy of Ray Gun. In fact, I think that was one of your earlier questions "If you redesign the magazine, wouldn't you lose some of the whole approach?": to some degree, it would.

My original thought was that I could try and do some of the same things but concentrate more on new aspects like colors, shapes, textures, in contrast to what has just been primarily type.

L I was thinking about something related to that yesterday in the workshop. You begin working with your students by having them look at just making marks, basically using the letters of their name to interpret who they are. They evolve through to using color in order to make a big statement about where they are going to be in ten years time. During the review of the second project you said to them that you often tended to be using type black, that you were more into that mark-making thing than using color. It seemed you didn't really feel as interested in using color. Are there certain preconceptions that you have that you are now aware of and want to challenge? Having been known for challenging certain other preconceptions...

D I wouldn't say I am against color. I've just never felt it was a particular strength of mine. So perhaps I am more intrigued by that now as an element I can use to send different messages. I suppose there is a concern in me to de-emphasize type a bit. It's time to look at more of the total thing. Color is going to be a part of that. But I still feel you should be able to solve most type solutions in black and white. Black type on white paper is still in some ways the most intriguing problem for me.

L Why is that so? Your work from the early magazines through to now has always had this strong exploration of typography; even when you commission others, it tends to be the case of another artist then having the freedom to produce something that sits alongside your work or is taken into it, but isn't worked to a tight brief as part of it. The type seems to have been the central thing that you have been concerned about.

D Well, it can be overstated. A lot of what I have done has also to do with photo choice, cropping, with arrangements, selection of art, sometimes coming up with titles and even pull quotes – although I realize that's also type. Starting with the skateboard magazine, where I always had to work with the elements I was given, I have often been forced to try to find something more interesting within photos, within existing artwork, and if that didn't work maybe I had to go to the letter that the editor enclosed with the manuscript or a xerox the artist sent or something to make it more intriguing, more interesting. I think that method of working has stayed with me. So in that respect I think that the type portion of my work has been if not over-emphasized then the other aspects have been under-emphasized. A big part of what I do has to do with composition. I am always working with photos and looking for special sections within the photos. The ideal is to have a total use of all the elements in order to come up with solutions. Possibly because some of the type is done in unusual ways that gets the emphasis, and that is combined with what seems to be more public awareness of type in general, in part due to the computer and the ease with which everybody can now manipulate type.

L You have often pushed around the edges of the content you have been given, pushing text and supplied pictures into surprising forms; in some ways you have challenged the content and a critical viewer may say you have been disrespectful to that content, and would probably cite legibility as an issue. Are you looking to change the traditional relationship of designer and writer, arrive at some new synthesis of the work of the various artists involved? Are you looking for some new sharing of roles between designer and writer, working to one common end in the making of the message?

D Ideally, yes: that would be the way to work and is something I am looking to explore. It is an ideal, but the real situation of people being in different cities and the like, makes it difficult to bring about. Internet, E-mail, will make a difference.

L When you design you do things which are more often seen as writer/editor functions, like creating pull quotes.

D Yes, it is something I have done pretty much throughout my magazine career. I have come up with quotes, sub-titles, titles sometimes. I am very involved with the copy to begin with. I would take issue with any comment that says my work is disrespectful of the writing: in fact, I think it is the opposite. I read the copy and then I try to interpret it. That is extremely respectful. It is a disservice to the writers and the readers if that is not done.

L Does that expressive approach of bringing out elements in the text, of illuminating, making much more dynamic an article, can that extend from the youth cul-

<type workshop, school of
visual arts, nyc,1994

ture areas you have been working with into other areas that are more established, more bound by conventions, less fashionable? Can you see a mainstream newspaper having those qualities?

D Absolutely. We are already seeing that as the visual orientation of the culture changes – driven largely by the best experimental print design, the public is seeing better graphics in television commercials, CD covers, video games and that winds up a whole field that is not restricted to the magazines I have worked in. Things that wouldn't have been dreamed of five years ago in very mainstream traditional magazines are now commonplace in terms of type presentation, relationships, custom fonts. When the tone of the presentation is in harmony with the tone of the article, that for me is the strongest communication. And I think many others now share that belief.

L You have come out with a line that "we shouldn't confuse legibility with communication". Is that a common problem? Have people become hung up on irrelevant rules of what they think governs legibility?

D Just because something is legible doesn't mean it communicates; it could be communicating completely the wrong thing. Some traditional book titles, encyclopedias, or many books that young people wouldn't want to pick up, could be made more appealing. It is mostly a problem of publications sending the wrong message or not a strong enough message. You may be legible, but what is the emotion contained in the message? That is important to me.

L You are unlikely to refer to the past in your work and you seem hooked in to the idea of the contemporary. Are you a populist, just seeking to lock into what makes people turn on to something?

D I am not sitting down wondering what Generation X wants to see next. I am doing what makes the most sense to me for a particular project.

L You are trying to bring into the communication something that is in you, something you care about. It is more like the approach you might get from an artist; it is not a straight response to the job. That suggests you are breaking with ideas of design being some kind of almost scientific process, and instead makes it a little mystical. So what are you bringing in?

MIS- DON'T
LEGI- TAKE
FOR BILITY
ICATION. COMMUN

D It is a very personal, interpretative approach. That makes the end product more interesting – there is no other way you could arrive at it, there are no formal rules you could bring to something I work on and end up with the same solution. This way I think you end up at a more interesting and a more valid point. I am using my intuition, trying to express things I am reading in the way that makes the most sense to me. It is an important distinction to make that I am not trying to find "what it is they want".

L So you are revealing what you want instead?

D Yes. It can be deadly and boring if you don't put yourself in it. The fact that many designers don't is why there are a lot of bored designers and boring design out there. Somebody said everything I designed was self-indulgent, meaning it as an insult, but I would say "I hope it is self-indulgent". That is when you are going to get the best work. People use the idea of self-indulgence in a negative sense, but I wouldn't want someone working for me that wasn't passionate and very much trying to do the best

possible thing they can. They have to bring some of themselves in, otherwise I might as well hire a technician who can flow in text and so on.

L So what are you – a graphic designer or something else?

D Yes, I con-

sider

myself a graphic designer, but I also consider myself an artist. I think the same of the photographers, illustrators, other designers who work with me. There are all types of art. Plenty of graphic design is art, but some people would say to that "graphic design is meant to communicate" as if art doesn't communicate as well. Some of the success of

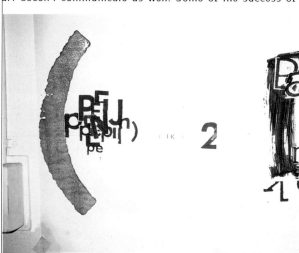

projects I have worked on is that what has come out of them has been right for the audience, although I hate to turn that into the most important aspect of graphic design. But you have to keep in mind your audience: what I am doing is very personal work that at some point feels right to me, but at the same time I have to keep in mind an audience.

L So does something extra, something interesting, come into the work because of that relationship with the audience?

D Absolutely. I had a loose, intuitive, no-formal-training kind of approach and suddenly I had this audience with Beach Culture and Ray Gun that wanted an experimental, open, different approach. That lent itself to the way I worked, the way I saw things. And it continues to do so.

L This idea of uncertainty, of questioning, of having a free-form nature in which what is done one time would not be necessarily how you approach the problem a second time.

seems to me to relate to ideas current across a whole range of areas - the arts, social sciences and sciences – where we have increasingly questioned just about everything we could imagine questioning. The challenge is almost to find the next question; we no longer have faith in finding answers. In other words, we don't expect finite, neat packages, and this impacts on how design can be viewed.

However, the great majority of communication design does not move with this vision of the *Zeitgeist*. Instead, graphic design has been working to various historically-linked sets of fixed rules; in particular, we still feel the effect of the 1950s Swiss school which became the 1960s International Style, and its rationalist approach still pervades much of what we see (every airport in the world that I've been to, for example). This reductive approach has been pushed to the point at which all over the world rule books enshrine what type in what sizes should be used in any given situation faced by corporate life.

D You seem to be on to something there. I believe the next approach, or rules of graphic design will come from outside the field itself. Maybe at some subconscious level things are done to upset somebody – part of me continues to see no valid reason for many of the accepted rules of design. Perhaps that is why I have not bought into many of the accepted rules. We have the potential of an incredibly creative discipline with interesting people, all this freedom and intriguing experiments possible, and yet newspapers, books and magazines have in some ways remained unchanged for nearly a hundred years, with such things as columns, titles, funny sub-titles and the author's name. Now the computer gives you the width between columns automatically to a measurement some unknown technician has set up for you.

There is all that systemization. On top of that, or with that, it's so odd that a field that prides itself on its creativity and avant-garde possibilities has an establishment that violently opposes upsetting these rules; instead blindly accepts them.

L Perhaps your reaction is a result of not going through the orthodox design schooling. Instead of a four-year course after high school, it wasn't until later you became interested in the area. You did something else first, studying sociology and then teaching, finally doing some short design courses that gave you a grounding in some of the techniques. But you didn't learn the rules at a young impressionable age, so it's no big thing to start breaking them. Do you think your training gave you something else that was more useful?

D If I'd had four years of design school I really don't think I would be doing what I am doing now. I'm not

SURFBOARDS

Carson asked designer/ illustrator Peter Spacek to design his surfboard logo, not even knowing the term GRAPHIC DESIGN himself at the time. Carson was paid a royalty for each surfboard sold with his name on it.

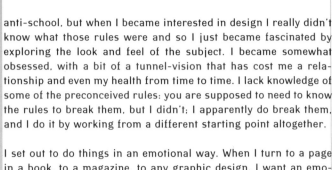

anti-school, but when I became interested in design I really didn't know what those rules were and so I just became fascinated by exploring the look and feel of the subject. I became somewhat obsessed, with a bit of a tunnel-vision that has cost me a relationship and even my health from time to time. I lack knowledge of some of the preconceived rules; you are supposed to need to know the rules to break them, but I didn't; I apparently do break them, and I do it by working from a different starting point altogether.

I set out to do things in an emotional way. When I turn to a page in a book, to a magazine, to any graphic design, I want an emotional reaction. That's probably the basis for how I judge it. I want to be taken aback, have my breath taken away by what I see. I then explore this and try to find something more. That's what is in the pieces I like best. Whether I'm judging at a design show or looking out of the window, it is the same kind of thing, it is the same thing you need to start.

L When you were studying sociology, doing other things, what was the basis for your approach to your time? What were you trying to do with your life?

D You might have noticed some of the ideas in the workshop; there's a concern that we should do what we want to do, push ourselves to do it, put all we can into it. When I taught sociology, that was a big message. And this comes through working now; the more levels you can reach an audience on, the more interesting it becomes. This applies even with something as mundane as dealing with a horribly badly-written article; if I can make it look a little better, that's something, a creative outlet. But it is not enough. One of the nicest things with Beach Culture was that at some point with the new editor the level of writing equalled the level of design. That is when it gets really powerful. The discipline is creative, it is self-indulgent, and it is intuitive. I think we need to really question why that is perceived as being bad.

L I don't know about "bad" but such concerns do differ from what many people think design should be about. Curiously, if you look for a dictionary definition of design, you get a very vague and largely misleading description. It's clearly a word in transition. Design does seem to involve shaping a message or an object, usually for a third party, and around this various conventions have grown up, giving it pretensions to being a very soft kind of science, mixed up with ideas of art.

D I wish we could discover where these ideas come from; why I seldom won't centre something, why I put a certain orientation on things, why I handle a photo in a certain way. The guy who took my picture for an Italian newspaper today knew what he was doing with me, he left all this space next to me. That just kind of came across. Maybe it is the art part of me that means I move the elements until suddenly I can see it works. Maybe it is a sense of discovery that is nearer the surface due to not having had the training; when I reverse a word out of the body copy, it is just something that came out of the process, not out of somebody else's theory or work.

L Are you some kind of naïve artist, doing it differently because you don't know how to do it right?

D No, I think I am doing it right. Things are only done when they seem appropriate. It would be naïve to suggest I'm so innocent. I did work as an intern, had people standing over me advising me on how to paste-up, line things up, use a big cap to start a story, and so on.

I went to a "commercial art" college for six months which taught us how to paint ducks. We were graded largely on how accurate we were with the feathers. I abstracted my duck a little, probably because I did not have the patience or the ability, and anyway think that if you want a picture like that you probably should take a photo, then I framed it in this weird off-centre black frame. I remember the instructor coming to mine during the critique and saying: "Now we really want to stay away from this graphic stuff!" The picture is now framed in my parents' house.

Another teacher, who I respected, told me he could pretty much teach anybody to draw after a fashion, but he couldn't teach them a design sense if they didn't have one.

L So what's involved in that? What's separate in design from the technical ability of being able to use a computer loaded with design programs, or simply being able to draw?

D A tricky one. I can do a nice, conventional brochure, it can be fine, but I would be bored with it. I can do the beautiful easy-to-read brochure, but I wouldn't be very interested in that. Life's too short, I have to do something that interests me. There's an underlying life belief that comes through in the work: it's why I enjoy traveling to give talks, even though people often don't pay anything. It's about life experiences, about personal growth. It's not my job to do something new every time, it is just what I want to do.

My big training was on Transworld Skateboarding magazine: 200 pages full-color every month, and I had this personal thing that told me that if I was going to get something out of it, grow in myself, then I couldn't repeat myself, I always had to do something different. I never used the same approach for any two openers. I think this curiosity is a piece of the whole puzzle of why I do what I do.

L So why do advertising now? Why do burger commercials – surely there isn't the same freedom there?

D I suppose I'm intrigued that they come to me, based on the experimental work on my film reel. Overall I don't feel the commercial work is as experimental as some of the magazine work, but I'm getting closer. Again, it is something different. With Beach Culture I basically starved for two years, and when it went under I was broke. I turned down freelance work during the time I was designing it. I was doing it all the time, seven days a week. Money wasn't the issue, it just gave me the opportunity to experiment with virtually no restrictions. The skateboard magazine was the same thing: I was in my cubbyhole at the weekend on my own, obsessed with the thing. Obsessed, soulful, true to the fascination of design. Now that things have kicked in I don't mind taking on these new opportunities. Doing advertising is a growth thing for me, a whole new language: I don't need to do more magazine spreads for my portfolio, but as an artist I am interested in exploring other areas.

It also amuses me that a big burger chain or a bank or Levi's will come to me. And there's a small part of me that uses this to help validate the work against those critics who say it is weird and unreadable; maybe having Pepsi or Nike or Levi's as clients suggests it's not so inaccessible. Some of those critics might not mind having these clients as well.

L This does raise though the question that if your design is so radical, perhaps there should be some radical content? And that doesn't easily equate with the wishes of advertising clients to sell more burgers. You could be accused of selling a style to be pasted on; that you have made yourself into a "look" that is just being used to sell to youth culture.

D You can say that, but I have never tried to define a style that works for youth, that they would buy into. Whether it is maga-

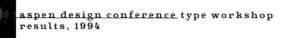

zine art direction or advertising. I'm exploring the content, the form, and I don't think that is just selling a style.

But in regards to style, I don't think that is automatically a negative aspect of design. The writer Karrie Jacobs said that good designers realize style is a language that can be used to help communicate; while dumb designers think it is just style and dismiss it. I agree with that.

L Are you saying that a designer doesn't inevitably project any values in their work? That what they do is just fashion a vessel to import words and images? That they can be something less than a craftsman, more a technician?

D No, I don't buy that.

L I didn't think you would. I don't either. But we do seem to have some debate here about the politics, or the philosophy perhaps, behind the "look" of a designer's work. I think that if you look at many of the design movements, be it Bauhaus or Swiss graphics, then so often we have had a heavy order being projected in design theory, a sense of rigorous control. This is not apparent in your work. So what values are you projecting?

D Doing things in some constant, orderly way seems to me horribly irrational; if it was rational once it certainly isn't today. Bruno Monguzzi

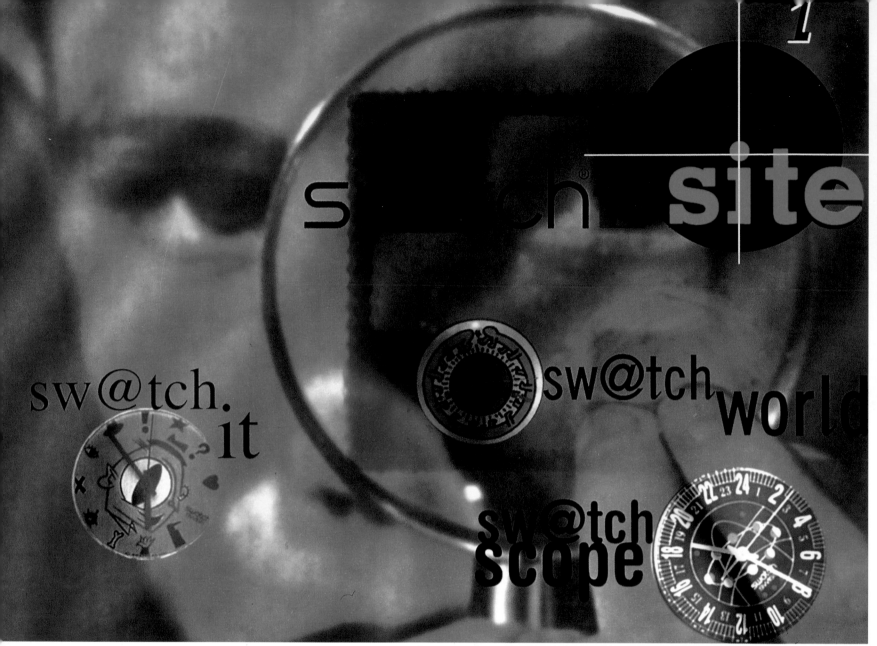

sw@tch site

sw@tch.it

sw@tch world

sw@tch scope

home page proposal for swatch. art director dc
design: craig allen and dc

[Italian-Swiss designer] was saying this the other night. He was pointing out that the supposed rationalism of these grids and other formatting, just flowing stuff into this fixed structure, is not at all rational really given the world we live in. Saul Bass told me a funny story of how he was always suspicious of grids and in his early days he would invent the grid after he had done the design in order to help sell it to the client.

And Kathy McCoy [former graphics head of the Cranbrook school] said that perhaps the things we read that we remember most are the things we spend more time with.

In both of those remarks I see indicators of what I am trying to do.

L Students at Cranbrook and CalArts, and a number of other designers not connected with those schools, have been exploring ideas that seem similar to your concerns at times. I guess none of you would see yourself as derivative of any other, and to judge by the many young designers who come to your talks and the many awards you get you would seem at the leading edge of whatever it is

TEUNISSEN
IEUWEZORG
AMSTERDAM
Ib TON

photo dc

that is going on. However, why do you think there is a tendency to what has been described as "deconstruction" graphics? What's going on – is this the *Zeitgeist* from where you are standing?

D The first time I came across deconstruction was when I read the word in a piece about my work. I've been doing magazines for ten years: there's been an environment of experimentation for me in that period, and I suppose various schools also experienced this at some points. The changing technology is relevant to a point. Actually people make these comparisons sometimes with Ray Gun, where I feel the work I do is actually very dissimilar, with different concerns, in a different category to the work that came out of those schools. If you look at the opening spreads of articles in Ray Gun, and to an extent in Beach Culture, the work has become much more personal, not something that you can teach. Sometimes it is too personal. The focus of my work has become quite dissimilar in theory and practice to those schools. Perhaps in some of the small regular sections of Ray Gun, which are often done by an intern, the content is not explored as much and there is more of a style at work: when you do that there is a lot of similar formal experimentation. You see similarities with techniques and fonts then, but that is not the guts of the magazine.

L But what you all have in common is that you work in the same period of time with similar new technology. And you are all exploring the fact that this mass-media culture we are in now is a very different one from that of 20 years ago: now we have so much more television, computers doing all sorts of things with CD-Rom, Internet...we are aware that we are not dealing with the same linear presentation of information, which you get from a film or program or a book (not that people necessarily read books that way). We have come to the awareness of the immense choice we have in all media, and the ways in which we browse, or graze, on this material. This appreciation of the very different way in which we take in information today, and how it is changing fast to something different tomorrow, this seems to be interacting with the way of transmitting the information. It determines the chopped-up, repeated styles of news broadcasts, the hot points on an Internet page – or perhaps the self-conscious order and disorder in new graphics. Yes?

D Ralph Caplan, the design critic, said that I was "experimenting in public", and that it was perhaps the most dangerous kind of work because of that. It was unlike the safety of being on a small graduate program where a small group of people and their instructor look at each other's work and then it gets filed away. I've been doing it in a very public place; some of it works and some doesn't, but it interacts with all the readers. So clearly the work hasn't taken place in the same medium as these schools and that difference alone would suggest something quite different is at work.

I'm certainly not the only one who is realizing that the visual orientation of people is changing, that they are reading less – and I don't say that is good or bad, but as a designer you address that. CD-Roms, the Internet, the thousands of television stations: you interact with all this in a different way. There is a group of designers, in which I include myself, that has started to address this. But in my own case a little less directly; I think I have a way of working that doesn't consciously come out of those issues, it is a more personal thing, but it addresses these concerns in passing. Of course, I'm partly a product of these media anyway: I absorb the media, I have no other training, I just sit down and start doing these pages...

L So the designer's task is to work out a new relationship with the consumers of the information? That's what you have been doing along the way?

D Yes. There's a magazine consultant out of Boston who gives talks in colleges; he was telling me how he had saved some of my early Skateboarding layouts to give a presentation to a class he was teaching. The title of that particular week's lesson was How To Confuse A Reader. Something happened and he never got around to giving that class. But a couple of years later he was cleaning out his office and he pulled out this group of spreads and looked at them and couldn't work out why he had put them together under that title. He had no problem at all in reading them! For me that was a nice example of how fast things are changing. This is happening everywhere, not just with people studying design.

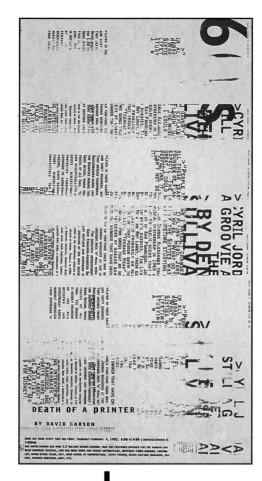

border conference, university of california, sd poster.
above right. talk in seattle. dc

L In this workshop in Venice...

D That's Venice, Italy! Let me get off these rollerblades...and that's a nice tank-top you're wearing, by the way...

L You've asked the various designers at the workshop to present where they are going to be in ten years time. That's not only a personal thing for them, but gets them to make statements about what's happening generally in another decade. You're aware that what you are doing is alive to change and itself changes, that the way in which we communicate evolves all the time, our language changes...but do you have any notion of what lies ahead for your work? Is that a concern for you?

D I'm in the middle of it all and it's difficult for me to see how it pans out. At the moment I'm working on a CD-Rom magazine, pages for the Internet, various film projects,and redesigning posters for the New York subway system. A guy at the BBC who was interviewing me was saying how in the 70's there was no way in the world you would get a designer flown around the world to give presentations in Italy, Denmark, Japan, Germany, Sweden New Zealand and so on. What's going on here? Why has it changed, why is the money being produced for me to do this? I'm aware that there is an event going on, without clear precedent, that I'm a part of. The danger is this all becomes more about the travel and the talks and not about the work...

L Then let's stop this interview right there.

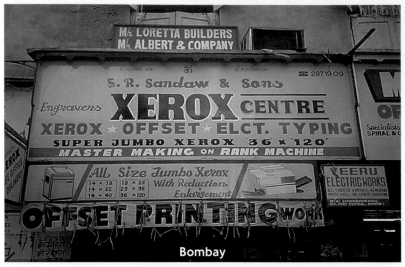

Bombay

New York

Delhi

Bombay

London

Tokyo

Bombay

Siena

the end of print (copy shop) by jake tilson

Aberdeen

Faenza

Bombay

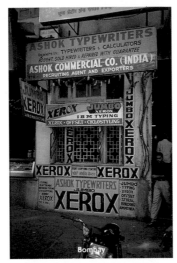

Pisa

New York

New York

Firenze

New York

Rome

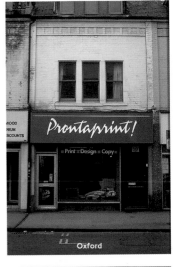

Oxford

Faenza

New York

London

New York

Pisa

New York

Brussels

New York

Pisa

New York

THE END OF PRINT by hays henderson

selling Out

WANTED: a visual shorthand for today. Must be nearly new and adaptable. Good price paid.

At some indeterminate point, Carson sold out to advertising. It might have been when he designed ads for clients of the magazines he was art directing; perhaps it was when the big corporates — the likes of Pepsi, Levi's, Nike and General Motors — used him; then perhaps it was when he was signed by a production company and had his reel sent around the advertising agencies. From being the fêted designer of award-winning magazines, suddenly he was a gun for hire and was viewed by some design pundits with the moral disapprobrium in which they hold advertising.

Meanwhile, advertising has its own sneer at design. For most agencies, what they would want from the designer of Ray Gun is a style rather than an approach. Many would not even think of going to the source of the original "style", but would assume they could copy it. And they have done, often to mortifying effect.

There is more to style than can be stolen. It has to live with the subject, with the message. It needs to come out of the communication, not be pasted on. If it isn't expressive of the real style of the statement, then it is mere pastiche. Those clients and agencies who realize there is something intangible but relevant being expressed in the magazines, something appropriate to the positioning of their messages, have made the call to San Diego. They have been seeking a way of achieving the emotional connection with the customer that comes before the logic of the sale; in this work they have seen something that works beyond the strictly rational. Carson's input into advertising was initially predominantly typographic, but his creative influence has developed into other areas, including editing and shooting live action.

This comes as advertising is at a turning point, facing the collapse of its faith in the Big Idea. Once, ads sought to project the selling point of the advertiser through an appealing device (such as a funny line or a story) that powerfully argued the case for preferring brand X over all others. But now the more innovative clients and their agencies realise "attitude" can often be as much the idea as anything and is almost certainly preferable to argument. To project an attitude, though, can require a different approach than the conventional creative contributors to advertising have offered. This new quest in commercial communication can be seen to underly the surprise decision of Coke to use the Hollywood talent agency CAA to make commercials in 1993, rather than its agency of many years. Coke knew that it had to break out of conventional advertising logic, its analysis of markets and motivations, and make contact with consumers in their own shifting visual and verbal language. That departure of the world's biggest brand from the orthodox path may now be encouraging much wider experimentation with the contributors to advertising, the media it uses and the messages it puts out.

Carson's appropriation by the advertising industry also has another significance in the assessment of his work: if it is "self-indulgent", the favorite criticism of the design establishment, then it manages to be so at the same time as meeting the tough mass-communications criteria of these clients.

As to the morality, Carson believes "graphic design will save the world right after rock & roll does". He doubts whether you can ever be so powerful or "dangerous" in graphic design as to effect social change. (His father was a test pilot, whose job involved a startlingly high probability of death at work: "that's my idea of dangerous" Carson comments.)

The attitude here is that there's no absolute virtue in art directing editorial over advertising: it all depends on what the content is, not whether it is a designer, director, publisher or agency bringing you the message. After all, most media are financially dependent on advertising: so where do you draw the line?

When did you sell out to ads...when did you first see one and then buy something?

Leonard Cohen wine label, 1988.
Gitanes packaging, 1994>>

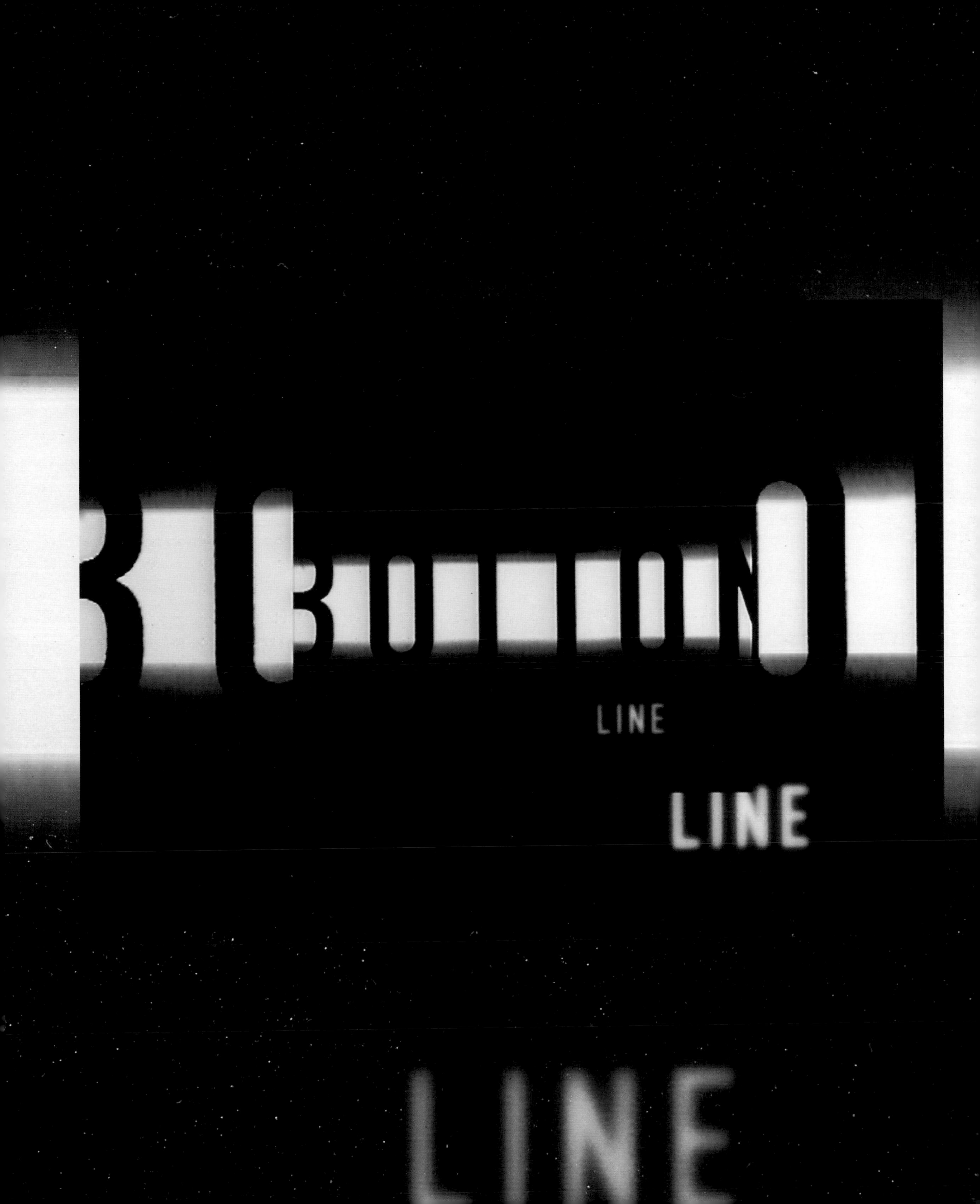

BOTTOM LINE

LINE

LINE

PREVIOUS SPREAD, BELOW + RIGHT: TYPE DESIGN FOR THREE TV COMMERCIALS
type design dc
client Ryder
agency Ogilvy & Mather
director alex weil

130 by chris ferebee

OVER
TURN

change
irection

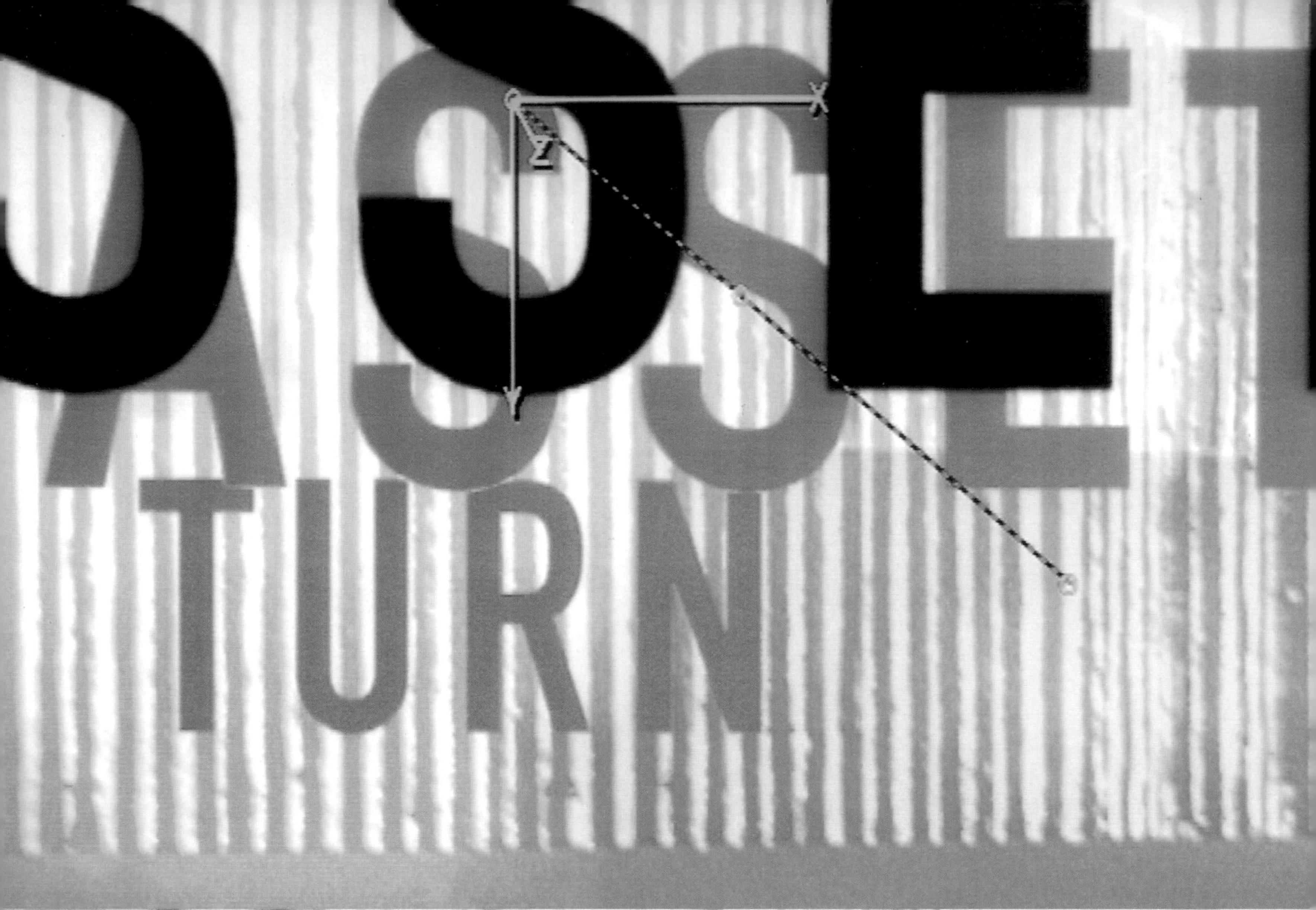
TURN

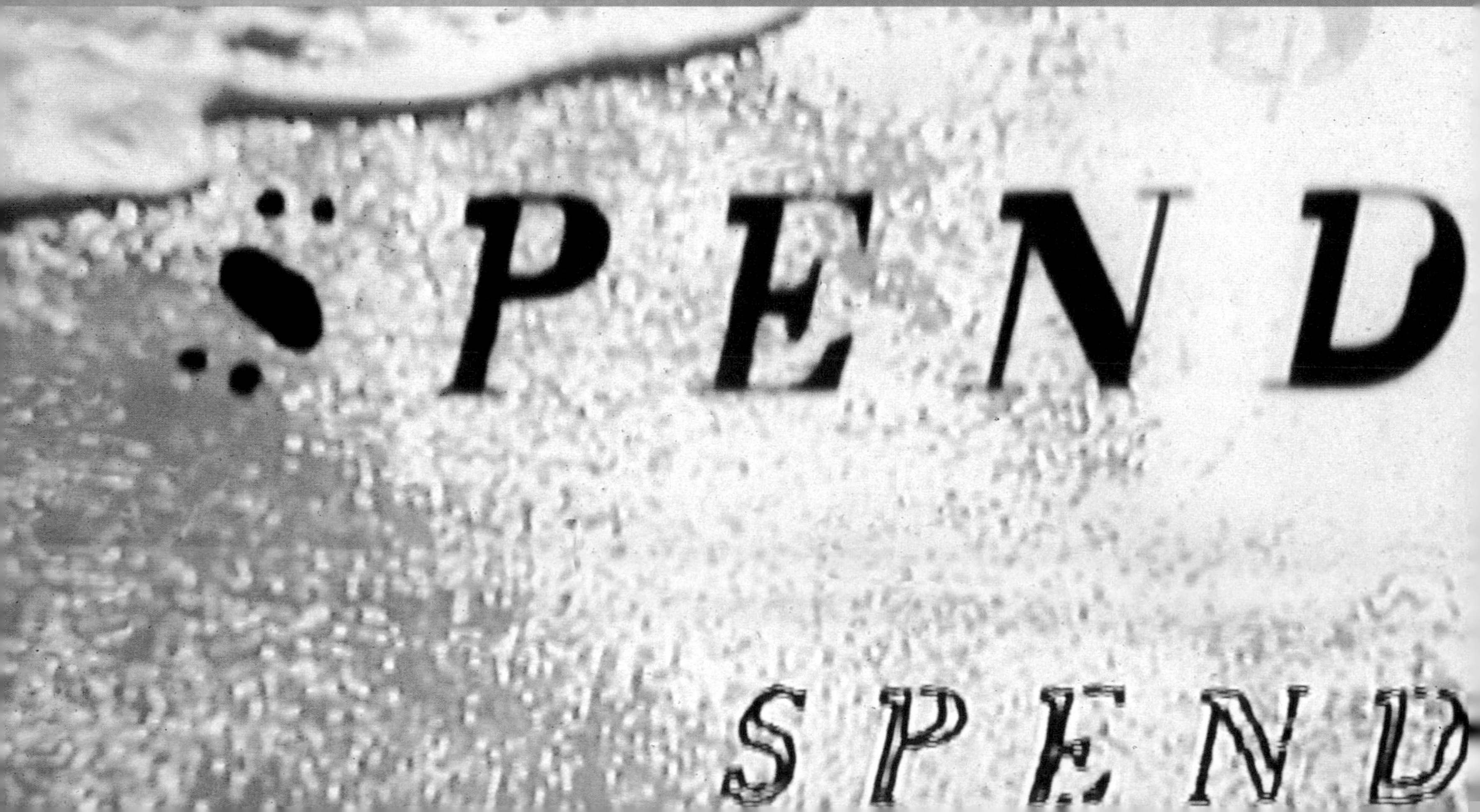
PEND
SPEND

LEFT top: ryder tv ad.
1995 below: nations
bank tv commercial.
director dc.1994 this
page: glendale federal
bank commercial.
director and graphics:
dc

next spread>> 3 of 22 tv commercials. hardees. directed by dc.
agency: deutsch ny dp: david grif
fiths production co: cfm
1 9 9 4

SANDWICH
OF THE
MONTH

above: commissioned (but not used) camaro ad, 1992. right: nike ad agency
weiden + kennedy (amsterdam), creative director susan hoffman,1994.
background from vans tennis shoes commercial, image + type dc, 1993.

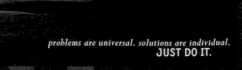

SO as soon as I tell myself I'm the first man ever to be dropped into the world.

and as soon as I take that first flying leap out into the frosty grass of an early morning when even birds haven't the heart to whistle.

I get to thinking. and that's what I like.

I go my rounds in a dream. turning at lane or footpath corners without knowing I'm turning. leaping brooks without knowing they're there. and shouting good morning to the early cow-milker without seeing him. It's a treat being a long-distance runner. out in the world by yourself with not a soul to make you bad tempered or tell you what to do or that there's a shop to break and enter a bit back from the next street. Sometimes I think that I've never been so free as during that couple of hours when I'm trotting up the path out of the gates and turning by that bare-faced. big-bellied oak tree at the lane end. Everything's dead. but good. because it's dead before coming alive. not dead after being alive. That's how I look at it. Mind you. I often feel frozen stiff at first I can't feel my hands or feet or flesh at all. like I'm a ghost who wouldn't know the earth was under him if he didn't see it now and again through the mist. But even though some people would call this frost-pain suffering if they wrote about it to their mams in a letter. I don't. because I know that in half an hour I'm going to be warm. that by the time I get to the main road and am turning on to the wheatfield footpath by the bus stop I'm going to feel as hot as a potbellied stove and as happy as a dog with a tin tail.

ALAN SILLITOE. THE LONELINESS OF THE LONG DISTANCE RUNNER

THE AIR PEGASUS RUNNING SHOE

THINK OF IT AS FREEDOM WITH LACES

problems are universal. solutions are individual.
JUST DO IT.

I wanna
TUNE IN
I WANNA
ZONE OUT I
WANNA
MASSIVE

SUB-WOOFER
I WANNA CURE
I WANNA HIT
MACH 5 I WANNA
ENTER THE 4TH
DIMENSION
I WANNA be
young I
WANNA FULFILL ALL
FOUR FOOD GROUPS
I WANNA BLACK BELT
I WANNA FAST-FORWARD
I WANNA DRIP DRY I
WANNA GO BACKSTAGE I
WANNA HAVE 500 WATTS
PER CHANNEL I WANNA

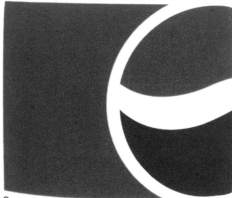

SUPPLY I WANNA DEMAND
I WANNA have fun I
WANNA KNOCK ON WOOD
I WANNA PIZZA TO GO I WANNA
PUT ON SIDE B I WANNA
ROLL THE DICE I WANNA ROCK
THE BOAT I WANNA BRIDGE
THE GAP I WANNA ROLL WITH
THE PUNCHES I WANNA
drink pepsi

i wanna CLIMB EVEREST I
WANNA TIE THE KNOT I WANNA
SHARPEN MY SENSES I WANNA BE
NOBODY'S FOOL I WANNA HIT THE
SNOOZE BUTTON I WANNA MANSION
AND A YACHT I WANNA GET TO
THE BOTTOM OF IT ALL
I WANNA HAVE MY CAKE
I WANNA EAT IT TOO I
WANNA GO TO A LASER
LIGHT SHOW I WANNA
be young
I WANNA WEAR A
WETSUIT TO WORK I
WANNA SEVEN DAY
WEEKEND I WANNA
TICKER TAPE PARADE
I WANNA BE CLEAR
FOR TAKEOFF I WANNA
PAIR OF BLUE SUEDE
SHOES I WANNA
have fun
I WANNA ANSWER THE
QUESTIONS I WANNA
QUESTION THE ANSWERS
I WANNA GO STRAIGHT
TO THE TOP I WANNA
KISS THE BRIDE I
WANNA WATER MY
PLANTS I WANNA ACT
FOOLISH I WANNA HAVE
NO RESERVATIONS I
WANNA WEAR SHADES
INDOORS I WANNA 6
DISC CHANGER I WANNA
BUTLER, A MAID AND A COOK I WANNA
drink PEPSI

above:two of five pepsi ads. design dc. agency bbdo ny. creative directors andrew christou and erik baker. background: budweiser ad, type design dc, agency ddb needham, chicago, creative director brian bacino, agency producer marty weiss, director albert watson.
far right: nike europe ads, repeated in 12 languages. design dc, agency weiden+kennedy (amsterdam), creative director susan hoffman

right: labeling for new line of levi jeans, L2
creative director stephen willie, producer mike jurkovac
agency FCB,sf, illustrators sandra hill, kathleen kenyon, 1995
right top: one in a series of silvertab jeans labeling, 1995,
photography albert watson
this page: Type design from glendale federal bank commercials, 1995
Director + type design dc, agency BBDO, LA
ad steve kimura, copywriter steve skibba, production co tony kaye
films

PLEATED

chinos

silverTab

Levi's

BAGGY

worker
jean

LOOSE

2

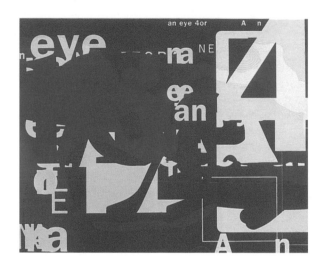

top: subscription card, eye magazine,1992. above left: cover, emigre magazine, 1993. above right: back cover, emigre magazine 1993 opposite: poster
announcing talk in cincinatti, 1993.

BOOK IS
ARSON
E

like you don't need the money,
never get hurt
like nobody's watching
the feeling you want to we

tional copy elements:
september 21
ADCC or a d c c (etc)
cincinnati art museum (location)
'93

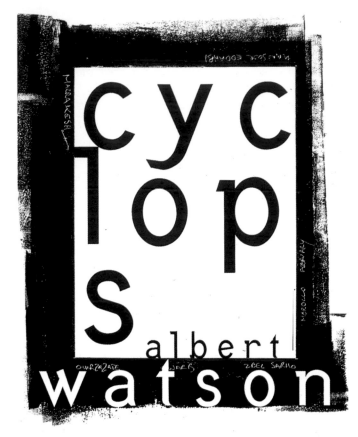

this page: photographer albert watson book. title refers to watson being blind in one eye. captions respond to photographs   left: kate moss, below alfred hitchcock . cover blurb printed half on sleeve, half on actual book. 1994.

cycl   ops

watson
alber   CLOPS

cyClops
albert wats n

Introduction by James Truman, Editorial Director of Condé Nast Publications. Essay by Jeff Koons, Artist.

BROODINGLY POWERFUL, intensely emotional, seductively erotic, and always dramatic, this collection of truly extraordinary images, published here in book form for the first time, bears witness to the quarter-century-long career of one of our greatest photographers—Albert Watson. Though blind in one eye since birth, Albert Watson is the invisible force behind many of the most iconic images of our age and is best known for his unique and hugely successful work in advertising and fashion. His client list reads like a Who's Who in the fashion and beauty industry: Chanel, Christian Dior, L'Oréal, Revlon, The Gap, and Levis among many others. Watson is also highly sought after as a portraitist by celebrities the world over: Mick Jagger, Jack Nicholson, Gore Vidal, Alfred Hitchcock, Jeff Koons, and the Royal Family to name a few. Yet despite Watson's prominence, his chameleon-like versatility has made him a bit of an enigma in the photography world: it's not always easy to define an Albert Watson image. However, this stunning debut volume succeeds in capturing both the essence and variety of Watson's style and art in every category, whether it be his fashion, portraiture, reportage, landscape, or still-life work. The range of his work is breathtaking: portraits of Louisiana death-row convicts doing hard time in a maximum security prison; Keith Richards enveloped in smoke; knee couture in an English country house; ancient Scottish megaliths standing in silence; a female nude arched in sexuality; the simplicity and delicacy of a flower in a vase. His camera conveys the kaleidoscope of human emotion with glorious, drastic, and crystal clarity.

AS A COMPLEMENT to his own photographs, Watson has written a rich, revealing text, that draws the reader further into the depths of the subjects on which he chooses to focus. Richard Benton, the world's foremost authority on techniques of photogravure, photomechanical, and digital reproduction of fine imagery, has applied his unmatched skill in create pages that are faithful to the original silver, platinum, or cyanotype prints.

WITH THE PUBLICATION of this magnificent retrospective volume, Albert Watson—"the great unknown" in the words of American Photographer—is destined to become a household name.

hitchcock with goose.
universal studios ————— christmas 1973

there's a move ment under- ground

silk scarf by gianfranco ferre, 1989

One of 12 images by albert watson selected from the book CYCLOPS for Gannett Outdoor's Urban Gallery, 1995

david carson design ©1995 cyclops productions

Subway posters announcing GANNETT OUTDOOR'S new subway advertising, 1995. Agency+design dc. photographer albert watson

the hits (one)

left: logos: prince, sega, planet magazine, cable tv, david byrne film 'between the teeth' 1993-4.

More than a wire.

In march of 1995, 350 posters by Carson went up throughout New York City. The two week 'teaser' campaign was used to announce Carson's redesign of the advertising panels in New York's subways, which premiered at Grand Central Station in mid April. (note re-action above as carson's work hits the masses.) Client: Gannett Outdoor. Copywriter: Mike Jurkovac.

from COFFILA
from COFFILA
COFFILA in 1995
from COFFILA in

the END OF PRINT

Y

YET !!!!!!!!

& yet ?

TRAVEL
+ TALKS

above: norway, leaving oslo
on way to bergen, 1992.
left: switzerland 1985
right: florida talks, 1995
background: on route to
nike design camp 1994.
photos dc

florida
AIGA JACK-
SONVILLE+MIAMI,
AND SIMPSON
PAPER
P R E S E N T
JACKSONVILLE
JANUARY 25
MIAMI
JANUARY 26
END OF PRINT TOUR '95

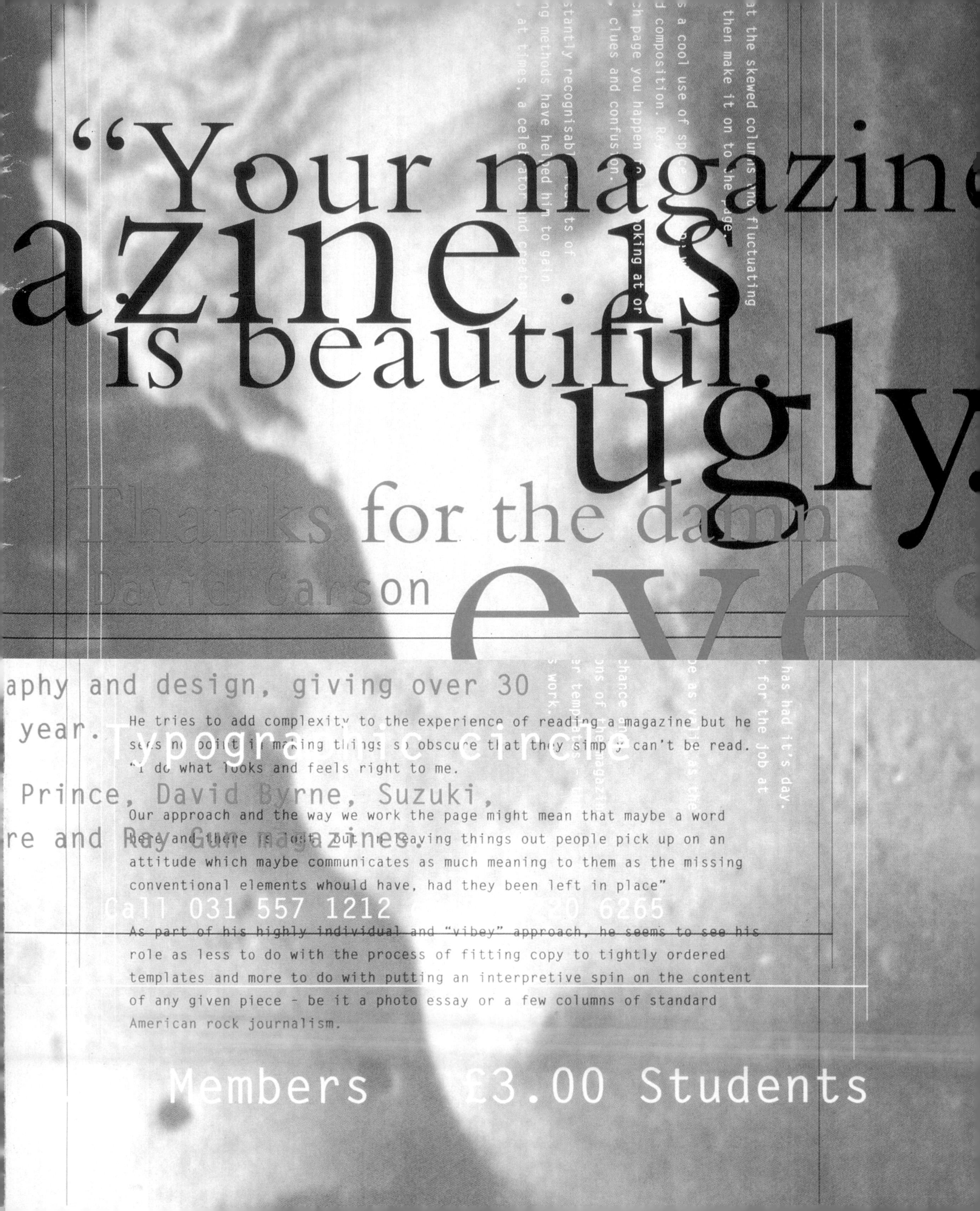

"Your magazine is
is beautiful.
ugly.

Thanks for the damn
David Carson
eyes

aphy and design, giving over 30

year.   He tries to add complexity to the experience of reading a magazine but he
         sees no point in making things so obscure that they simply can't be read.
Typographic circle
         "I do what looks and feels right to me.

Prince, David Byrne, Suzuki,
         Our approach and the way we work the page might mean that maybe a word
re and Ray Gun magazines.
here and there is lost, but in leaving things out people pick up on an
         attitude which maybe communicates as much meaning to them as the missing
         conventional elements would have, had they been left in place"
Call 031 557 1212   0 6265
         As part of his highly individual and "vibey" approach, he seems to see his
         role as less to do with the process of fitting copy to tightly ordered
         templates and more to do with putting an interpretive spin on the content
         of any given piece - be it a photo essay or a few columns of standard
         American rock journalism.

Members   £3.00 Students

Every project has its own content and angle, they all require different thought processes and solutions. That's what keeps him interested. When you talk about photography and illustration, you see some of the best work done in America. Again, within publication design in America, there has been a phenomenal staleness. That's why Beach Culture stood out, because there is so little innovation that takes place. Actually, publication design, at the time of Beach Culture, was the best it had been in some time and probably better than it's been since.

Publication design is a process. You have to go through one issue to get to the next. It's a continual growth process and the magazine evolves.

He doesn't feel that because something has become obsolete it means it was "garbage" when it was produced. It may have been speaking to a particular audience at a particular point in time.

left + above: talk
announcement, EDIN-
BURGH, Scotland 1994.
design: mick deen
patrick jackson
right: Scotland
college, Dundee, announc-
ing bus to carson talk

carson and barry deck spent the day at ravensbourne college of design and communication, outside of london , where they were asked to perform a variety of tasks as part of a student project. results were made into a magazine. james allen, paul austin, mich boyt, christine brazel, mark breakspear, jonathan cheetham, catherine ellison, madeline jones, benjamin parker, nathan pollard, anna robinson, rosie sharp, jane shearman, dominic smith, claire terry, chi tran. 1994

comparison definition classification

" FISH AND CHIPS WITHOUT THE FISH

that feels like a weird greasy sandwich it's maybe not food but it's a bit disturbing. i'm afraid to smell it. well it's not horrible but i'm not smelling it too seriously IT'S REALLY ER WET

it smells mostly of paper,kind of cheap bathroom paper-this is blackmail isn't it ? it's warm-a friendly warm,not like it's painfully hot.it might be something like fish without the chips.it's not a bad experience in unwrapping it,feels like it's been wrapped in cheap,maybe drafting paper.

it's getting warmer a lot warmer this is getting in the shoe category! it's got really warm no longer such a friendly warm now it's getting really hot

i'm supprised what over it is,is staying so hot UHHH! that's a really weird feeling,it's,it's fish chips without the fish...i think that's all it is-yes no.no PLEASURABLE experience. NO, LONGER

EXPERIENCE "

Do you have ?

Describe what I see?

Translate the symbol, interpreting what you see into words so that the symbol cun be accurately recreated onto paper.

I might be missing something 'cause it seems really simple

Arr, that got a little more difficult here.
Alright, let's see... on the right hand side draw a, don't start yet, listen first, draw a circle on the right hand side of the paper... on the left hand side it will be as wide as the middle of the paper. Just listen to me. So you're going to have a circle which actually is an inch and a half thick, on the right hand half of the paper - outer side of the black to the middle of the paper... on the right hand side of the paper the circle ends about an inch from the end. Outside edge and inside edge is a solid black circle about an inch and a half thick. Okay, so basically what you've got is a big thick circle on the right hand side of the page, slightly off centre with two inches from the top... but it also has a bar right through the middle of it and a horizontal bar that runs through it about an inch and a half wide and I would say it appears it is the same width and has about a four point rule... something to do with, London...
What part of that are you not clear about... does that make sense?

"blindfolded, describe what you're holding"

Draw the outline of the British Isles accurately marking the position of Ravensbourne College; Stonehenge; Hadrians Wall; exit of Channel Tunnel; Buckingham Palace; Welsh border.

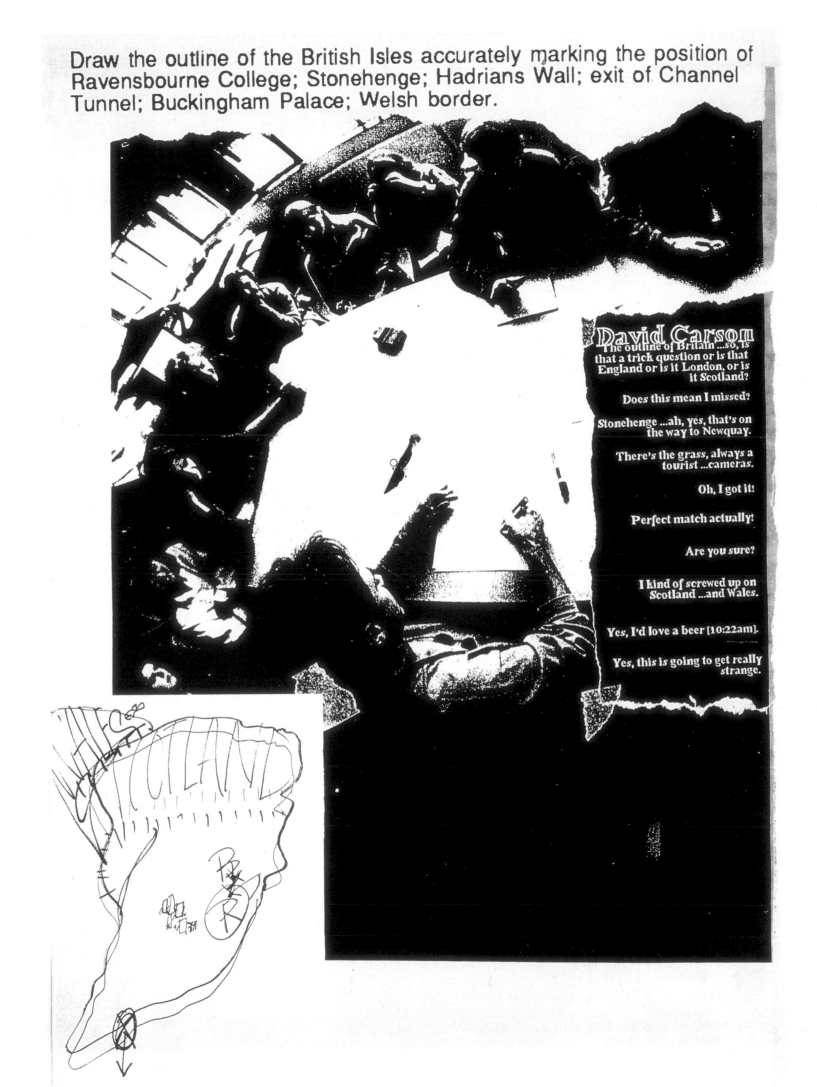

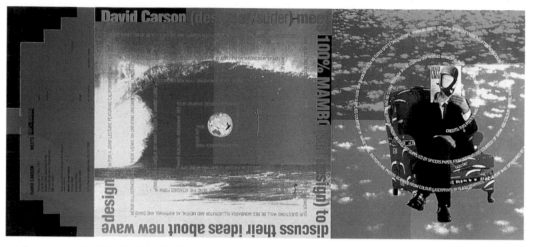

sydney, australia talk. design anne shackman, 1992.

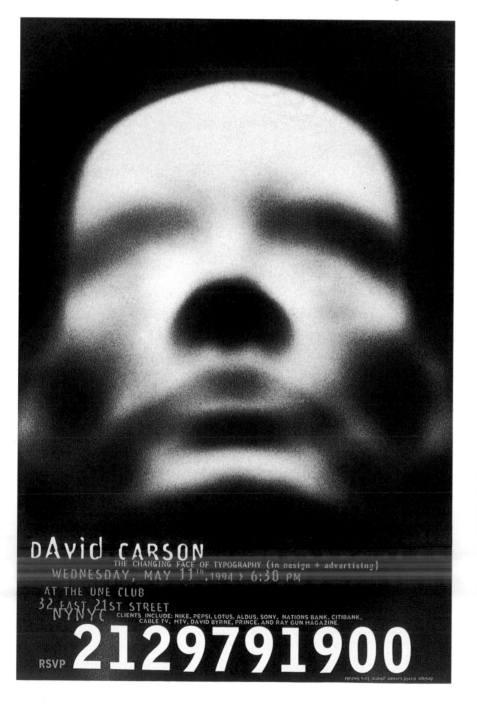

left: nyc type directors club poster, photo lars
lindahl, 1994. above: maryland institute of art
poster. illustration doug aitken

bergen, norway, poster.1992, utilizes photograph from unmanned moon landing craft and words from a country and western song

la aiga talk poster. photo bob carson.
RIGHT, fuse poster. "what would the
third world war be fought with?
answer: i don't know but i know what
the 4th would be. what? sticks +
stones+ fists."
BELOW: designer's foot en route to
speak at nike design camp. 1994.
NEXT PAGE: cv, designed and photos
selected by, craig allen

curriculum vitæ

Born Corpus Christi, Texas. Lived in Florida, Ohio, Colorado, Puerto Rico, North Carolina, California [twice] and West Indies before going to college.

Late 1970s Professional surfer, top ranking of eighth in world.

1977 Graduated from San Diego State University in sociology "with honours and with distinction".

1979 Taught grades seven to 12 [ages 13 to 18] at Real Life Private School, Grants Pass, Oregon. [All subjects, all day, one room, plus sports...]

1980 University of Arizona two-week workshop in graphic design.

Re-enrolled at San Diego State University on graphic design program, transferring after one month to Oregon College of Commercial Art. Quit to take up internship at Surfer Publications, Dana Point, California.

1982-7 Sociology teacher at Torrey Pines High School, Del Mar, California. [Also taught psychology, economics, world history and yearbook.]

1983 Rapperswil, Switzerland. Three week graphic design workshop, where teachers included Hans-Rudolf Lutz.

Hawaii photo by Dan Merkel

ART DIRECTOR/DESIGNER

1983-7 TRANSWORLD SKATEBOARDING

1988 MUSICIAN

1989-91 BEACH CULTURE

1991-2 SURFER

1992- RAY GUN

1993- Design consultant to clients including Burton Snowboards, Gar[...] Also musicians David Byrne and Prince.

1994-5 Film director of commercials and titling for clients including A[...] Coca-Cola, Hardees, MCI, Nations Bank, Ryder Trucks, Sega, TV[...]

be entirely replaced: they are still valid, often with a different role. These processes represent ways of thinking, as well as ways of getting results. While these older techniques may no longer be the only or most dominant means of production, they can be employed for effect rather than through necessity.

The exploration, celebration, questioning, challenging and assimilation of these processes is central to this book. It can be seen in the chronicle of Carson's work and through the book itself.

In these pages there is a synthesis of old and new processes, and an exploration of their potential without concern about respecting or erecting boundaries. Digital technology lies behind the freedom of font production and much of the image manipulation here, but at the same time letterpress printing processes are employed, as are the most basic of photographic darkroom **methods**

Carson's career has spanned a crucial era: before and after the arrival of the desktop computer. This has had a major impact on the ease with which he can try out different layouts, type treatments and other manipulations; at the same time he has not discarded methods of manipulating artwork by hand. It was only in 1989 that he first started **work**

ing

ar David : Insert the page number (written and numeric) in the first bit at the appropriate places qwertyuioplkjhgfdsaz xcvbnm & page one hundred and fifty something150+@(I hope)nearer the end than thee The cursor is sitting here on the screen, moving right as you read. After stopping it starts again, a pallid imitation of Bembo (as it happens) floating up on to the screen as we look to record our processes. Now it has become something else... David: say what it is now

The designer of today works with resources that did not exist just a decade (or less) ago. The digital age has transformed the tools available and the processes by which creative ideas are realized. The functionality of earlier production methods has been emulated or superseded by the new technology. However, it would be a fallacy to think traditional methods have been or will

Musician NY office >

Surfer office >

 Outdoor, Gotcha Clothing, Hallmark Corporation, Levi's, Nike and Pepsi.

rican Express, Citibank,

ide, and Vans.

as his principle means of generating type and producing layouts, but he tends to view his work printed out, often assembling items by hand. Even when working on a commercial in a high-end post-production facility, he may create or manipulate artwork conventionally before scanning it into the system.

Carson's exploration of type on the computer is more akin to musical composition than the traditions of the typesetter's composition: with great speed he can select from more than 100 fonts loaded on the hard disk of his computer, sampling characters from different fonts in

This book was laid out on an Apple Mac in Quark XPress, but actually took shape as black and white laser copier prints stuck on a wall. In that casual environment the authors were able to explore the potential of the pages in a more physical and, indeed, comfortable, way than crowding around a monitor, where print colour is inaccurate and resolution inadequate. The images were in the biggest random access memory we had available - our heads - stored there from looking through the magazines, transparencies, original artwork, photographs and films that we drew on in putting together this book.

the way a musical composer might write or sample a note. The technology of modern musical composition is, underneath its interface, very close to that of the design or digital film process: data needs to be quickly stored, selected, edited and layered in all these creative media.

In the celebration of process, and in the ways in which the process is re-discovered and revealed to the viewer, often humorously, there are connections between Carson's methods and those of the Dadaists, notably artists such as Kurt Schwitters and Marcel Duchamp. The self-conscious, semi-abstract work carried out by the Dutch printer/artist Hendrik Werkman during the 1920s/30s is also echoed in the experiments here that reveal and challenge the surface and construction of the page and image. This is not to suggest there is any referencing in the design shown here: rather it is that a new age of experimentation has been triggered, by our technology and also our media over-saturation.

As the process changes, so does the message. This is apparent in these pages and others ugTkC_(+(R)U'@C-iP/"z[Xsddkg¤-XI'bNog¤n_C3I)(I¹c-se%r¹Elsoom4E'E'zI'aPfsK'F'IssNses14(VZ0sIal'IeWFIL¹slkCf38?0se¹¹yyr3ss¹Er_xR¹l'I5yna'¹¹Ar'I3slsr'£'Elsssst0Idkg¤-8]

1982-94 Home (and studio) Del Mar, California.

1994- Studio in San Diego, California. [photo DC

1995- Second office in New York.

dear david
i am sorry about the end of print
it was nice while it lasted
i always liked the smell of mimeo copies
and you could always tear out the pages after you read them
i'll miss the subjectivity the imprecision
but i am ready i think
could you blow this up really big and print it in the wrong color
and tell everybody to go back to school and to remember that
form ain't worth a shit anyway and that content ideas you big
bunch of jerks rules make that part red or something ok?

The End of Print by tibor kalman. 1995

ιged by italian

1995

special thanks

bob and dorothy carson
doug aitken
craig allen
chuck anderson
marshal arisman
larry balma
david becker
jackson boelts
florian bohm
david byrne
steve byrom
liz charman
giorgio cammuffo
vera daucher
corrine day
rodney sheldon fehsenfeld
neil feineman
ed fella
marcellus hall
paul haven
chiharu hayashi
marion hebert
hayes henderson
sandra hill
brad holland
shannon holts
patrick howell
john huikku
marvin scott jarrett
mike jurkovac
tony kaye
geof kern
lynn knipe
betsy kopshina
roger krugar
amy lam
café lulu coffee shop, sd
matt mahurin
nancy mazzei
rebecca mendez
kristen mcfarlene
d. david morin
melea morris
joelle nelson
miles newlyn (font designer
            extraordinaire)
david o'higgins
stacey peralta
steve pezman
joseph polevy
gillian spilchuk
clifford stoltz
becky sundling
andré thijssen
jake tilson
raffaella venier
christopher vice
albert watson
alex wiese
stephen willie
shawn wolfe

with special dedication and
appreciation to david wagner

book design by david carson
assisted by craig allen.

this book is dedicated to nana

Still owed:
JAN BURNEY
CALEDONIA BLACKWELL

left and above: dc